Some Private Views

James Payn

Alpha Editions

This edition published in 2023

ISBN : 9789357968812

Design and Setting By
Alpha Editions
www.alphaedis.com
Email - info@alphaedis.com

Contents

THE MIDWAY INN.

'The hidden but the common thought of all.'

The thoughts I am about to set down are not *my* thoughts, for, as my friends say, I have given up the practice of thinking, or it may be, as my enemies say, I never had it. They are the thoughts of an acquaintance who thinks for me. I call him an acquaintance, though I pass as much of my time with him as with my nearest and dearest; perhaps at the club, perhaps at the office, perhaps in metaphysical discussion, perhaps at billiards—what does it matter? Thousands of men in town have such acquaintances, in whose company they spend, by necessity or custom, half the sum of their lives. It is not rational, doubtless; but then 'Consider, sir,' said the great talking philosopher, 'should we become purely rational, how our friendships would be cut off. We form many such with bad men because they have agreeable qualities, or may be useful to us. We form many such by mistake, imagining people to be different from what they really are.' And he goes on complacently to observe that we shall either have the satisfaction of meeting these gentlemen in a future state, or be satisfied without meeting them.

For my part, I do not feel that the scheme of future happiness, which ought by rights to be in preparation for me, will be at all interfered with by my not meeting again the man I have in my. mind. To have seen him in the flesh is sufficient for me. In the spirit I cannot imagine him; the consideration is too subtle; for, unlike the little man who had (for certain) a little soul,' I don't believe he has a soul at all.

He is middle-aged, rich, lethargic, sententious, dogmatic, and, in short, the quintessence of the commonplace. I need not say, therefore, that he is credited by the world with unlimited common-sense. And for once the world is right. He has nothing-original about him, save so much of sin as he may have inherited from our first parents; there is no more at the back of him than at the back of a looking-glass—indeed less, for he has not a grain of quicksilver; but, like the looking-glass, he reflects. Having nothing else to do, he hangs, as it were, on the wall of the world, and mirrors it for me as it unconsciously passes by him—not, however, as in a glass darkly, but with singular clearness. His vision is never disturbed by passion or prejudice; he has no enthusiasm and no illusions. Nor do I believe he has ever had any. If the noblest study of mankind is man, my friend has devoted himself to a high calling; the living page of human life has been his favourite and indeed, for these many years, his only reading. And for this he has had exceptional opportunities. Always a man of wealth and leisure, he has never wasted himself in that superficial observation which is often the only harvest of foreign travel. He despises it, and in relation to travellers, is wont to quote the famous parallel of the copper wire, 'which grows the narrower by going further.' A confirmed stay-at-home, he has mingled much in society of all sorts, and exercised a keen but quite unsympathetic observation. His very reserve in company (though, when he catches you alone, he is a button-holder of great tenacity) encourages free speech in others; they have no more reticence in his presence than if he were the butler. He has belonged to no cliques, and thereby escaped the greatest peril which can beset the student of human nature. A man of genius, indeed, in these days is almost certain, sooner or later, to become the centre of a mutual admiration society; but the person I have in my mind is no genius, nor anything like one, and he thanks Heaven for it. To an opinion of his own he does not pretend, but his views upon the opinions of other people he believes to be infallible. I have called him dogmatic, but that does not at all express the absolute certainty with which he delivers judgment. 'I know no more,' he says, 'about the problems of human life than you do' (taking me as an illustration of the lowest prevailing ignorance), 'but I know what everybody is thinking about them.' He is didactic, and therefore often dull, and will eventually, no doubt, become one of the greatest bores in Great Britain. At present, however, he is worth knowing; and I propose to myself to be his Boswell, and to introduce him—or, at least, his views—to other people. I have entitled them the Midway Inn, partly from my own inveterate habit of story-telling, but chiefly from an image of his own, by which he once described to me, in his fine egotistic rolling style, the position he seemed to himself to occupy in the world.

When I was a boy, he said (which I don't believe he ever was), I had a long journey to take between home and school. Exactly midway there was a hill with an Inn upon it, at which we changed horses. It was a point to which I looked forward with very different feelings when going and returning. In the one case—for I hated school—it seemed to frown darkly on me, and from that spot the remainder of the way was dull and gloomy; in the other case, the sun seemed always glinting on it, and the rest of the road was as a fair avenue that leads to Paradise. The innkeeper received us with equal hospitality on both occasions, and it was quite evident did not care one farthing in which direction we were tending. He would stand in front of his house, jingling his money—*our* money—in his pockets, and watch us depart with the greatest serenity, whether we went east or west. I thought him at one time the most genial of Bonifaces (for it was his profession to wear a smile), and at another a mere mocker of human woe. When I grew up, I perceived that he was a philosopher.

And now I keep the Midway Inn myself, and watch from the hill-top the passengers come and go—some loth, some willing, like myself of old—and listen to their talk in the coffee-room; or sometimes in a private parlour, where, though they speak low and gravely, their converse is still unrestrained, because, you see, I am the landlord.

Sometimes they speak of Death and the Hereafter, of which the child they buried yesterday knows more than the wisest of them, and more than Shakespeare knew. The being totally ignorant of the subject does not indeed (as you may perhaps have observed in other matters) deter some of them from speaking of it with great confidence; but the views of a minority would quite surprise you, and this minority is growing—coming to a majority. Every day I see an increase of the doubters. It is not a question of the Orthodox and the Infidel, you must understand, at all, though *that* is assuming great proportions; but there is every day more uncertainty among them, and, what is much more noteworthy, more dissatisfaction.

Years ago, when a hardy Cambridge scholar dared to publish his doubts of an eternal punishment overtaking the wicked, an orthodox professor of the same college took him (theologically) by the throat. 'You are destroying,' he cried, 'the hope of the Christian.' But this is not the hope I speak of, as loosing, and losing, its hold upon men's minds; I mean the real hope, the hope of heaven.

When I used to go to church—for my inn is too far removed from it to admit of my attendance there nowadays—matters were very different. Heaven and Hell were, in the eyes not only of our congregation, but of those who hung about the doors in the summer sun, or even played leap-frog over the grave-stones, as distinct alternatives as the east and west highways on each side of my inn. If you did not go one way, you must go the other; and not only so, but an immense desire was felt by very many to go in the right direction. Now I perceive it is not so. A considerable number of highway passengers, though even they are less numerous than of old, are still studious—that is in their aspirations—to avoid taking (shall I say delicately) the lower road; but only a few, comparatively, are solicitous to reach the goal of the upper.

Let me once more observe that I am speaking of the ordinary passengers—those who travel by the mail. Of the persons who are convinced that there never was an Architect of the Universe, and that Man sprang from the Mollusc, I know little or nothing: they mostly travel two and two, in gigs, and have quarrelled so dreadfully on the way, that, at the Inn, they don't speak to one another. The commonalty, I repeat, are losing their hopes of heaven, just as the grown-up schoolboy finds his paradise no more in home. I can remember when divines were never tired of painting the lily, of indulging in the most glowing descriptions of the Elysian Fields. A popular artist once drew a picture of them: 'The Plains of Heaven' it was called, and the painter's name was Martin. If he was to do so now, the public (who are vulgar) would exclaim 'Betty Martin.' Not that they disbelieve in it, but that the attractions of the place are dying out, like those of Bath and Cheltenham.

Of course some blame attaches to the divines themselves that things have come to such a pass. 'I protest,' says a great philosopher, 'that I never enter a church, but the man in the pulpit talks so unlike a man, as though he had never known what human joys or sorrows are—so carefully avoids every subject of interest save *one*, and paints that in colours at once so misty and so meretricious—that I say to myself, I will never sit under him again.' This may, of course, be only an ingenious excuse of his for not going to church; but there is really something in it. The angels, with their harps, on clouds, are now presented to the eyes, even of faith, in vain; they are still appreciated on canvas by an old master, but to become one of them is no longer the common aspiration. There is a suspicion, partly owing, doubtless, to the modern talk about the dignity and even the divinity of Labour, that they ought to be doing something else than (as the American poet puts it with characteristic ii reverence) 'loafing about the throne;' that we ourselves, with no ear perhaps for music, and with little voice (alas!) for praise, should take no pleasure in such avocations. It is not the sceptics—though their influence is getting to be considerable—who have wrought this change, but the conditions of modern life. Notwithstanding the cheerful 'returns' as to pauperism, and the glowing speeches of our Chancellors of the Exchequer, these conditions are far harder, among the thinking classes, than they were. The question 'Is Life worth Living?' is one that concerns philosophers and metaphysicians, and not the persons I have in my mind at all; but the question, 'Do I wish to be out of it?' is one that is getting answered very widely—and in the affirmative. This was certainly not the case in the days of our grand-sires. Which of them ever read those lines—

'For who, to dumb forgetfulness a prey,

This pleasing anxious being e'er resigned,

Left the warm precincts of the cheerful day,

Nor cast one longing lingering look behind?'—

without a sympathetic complacency? This may not have been the best of all possible worlds to them, but none of them wished to exchange it, save at the proper time, and for the proper place. Thanks to overwork, and still more to over-worry, it is not so now. There are many prosperous persons in rude health, of course, who will ask (with a virtuous resolution that is sometimes to be deplored), 'Do you suppose then that I wish to cut my throat?' I certainly do not. Do not let us talk of cutting throats; though, mind you, the average of suicides, so admirably preserved by the Registrar-General and other painstaking persons, is not entirely to be depended upon. You should hear the doctors at my Inn (in the intervals of their abuse of their professional brethren) discourse upon this topic—on that overdose of chloral which poor B. took, and on that injudicious self-application of chloroform which carried off poor C. With the law in such a barbarous state in relation to self-destruction, and taking into account the feelings of relatives, there was, of course, only one way of wording the certificate, but—and then they shake their heads as only doctors can, and help themselves to port, though they know it is poison to them.

It is an old joke that annuitants live for ever, but no annuity ever had the effect of prolonging life which the present assurance companies have. How many a time, I wonder, in these later years, has a hand been stayed, with a pistol or 'a cup of cold poison' in it, by the thought, 'If I do this, my family will lose the money I am insured for, besides the premiums.' This feeling is altogether different from that which causes Jeannette and Jeannot in their Paris attic to light their charcoal fire, stop up the chinks with their love-letters, and die (very disreputably) 'clasped in one another's arms, and silent in a last embrace.' There is not one halfpenny's worth of sentiment about it in the Englishman's case, nor are any such thoughts bred in his brain while youth is in him. It is in our midway days, with old age touching us here and there, as autumn 'lays its fiery finger on the leaves' and withers them, that we first think of it. When the weight of anxiety and care is growing on us, while the shoulders are becoming bowed (not in resignation, but in weakness) which have to bear it; when our pains are more and more constant, our pleasures few and fading, and when whatever happens, we know, must needs be for the worse—then it is that the praise of the silver hair and length of days becomes a mockery indeed.

Was it the prescience of such a state of thought, I wonder (for it certainly did not exist in their time), that caused good men of old to extol old age; as though anything could reconcile the mind of man to the time when the very sun is darkened to him, and 'the clouds return after the rain?' There is a noble passage in 'Hyperion' which has always seemed to me to repeat that sentiment in Ecclesiastes; it speaks of an expression in a man's face:

'As though the vanward clouds of evil days

Had spent their malice, and the sullen rear

Was with its storied thunder labouring up.'

This is why poor Paterfamilias, sitting in the family pew, is not so enamoured of that idea of accomplishing those threescore years and ten which the young parson, fresh from Cambridge, is describing as such a lucky number in life's lottery. The attempt to paint it so is well-meaning, no doubt, 'the vacant chaff well meant for grain;' and it is touching to see how men generally (knowing that they themselves have to go through with it) are wont to portray it in cheerful colours.

A modern philosopher even goes so far as to say that our memories in old age are always grateful to us. Our pleasures are remembered, but our pains are forgotten; 'if we try to recall a physical pain,' she writes (for it is a female), 'we find it to be impossible,' From which I gather only this for certain, that that woman never had the gout.

The folks who come my way, indeed, seem to remember their physical ailments very distinctly, to judge by the way they talk of them; and are exceedingly apprehensive of their recurrence. Nay, it is curious to see how some old men will resent the compliments of their juniors on their state of health or appearance. 'Stuff and nonsense!' cried old Sam Rogers, grimly; 'I tell you there is no such thing as a fine old man.' In a humbler walk of life I remember to have heard a similar but more touching reply. It was upon the great centenarian question raised by Mr. Thorns. An old woman in a workhouse, said to be a hundred years of age, was sent for by the Board of Guardians, to decide the point by her personal testimony. One can imagine the half-dozen portly prosperous figures, and the contrast their appearance offered to that of the bent and withered crone. 'Now, Betty,' said the chairman with unctuous patronage, 'you look hale and hearty enough, yet they tell me that you are a hundred years old; is this really true?' 'God Almighty knows, sir,' was her reply, 'but I feel a thousand.'

And there are so many people nowadays who 'feel a thousand.'

It is for this reason that the gift of old age is unwished for, and the prospect of future life without encouragement. It is the modern conviction that there will be some kind of work in it; and even though what we shall be set to do may be 'wrought with tumult of acclaim,' we have had enough of work. What follows, almost as a matter of course, is that the thought of possible extinction has lost its terrors. Heaven and its glories may have still their charms for those who are not wearied out with toil in this life; but the slave draws for himself a far other picture of home. His is no passionate cry to be admitted into the eternal city; he murmurs sullenly, 'Let me rest.'

It was a favourite taunt with the sceptics of old—those Early Fathers of infidelity, who used to occupy themselves so laboriously with scraping at the rind of the Christian Faith—that until the Cross arose men were not afraid of Death. But that arrow has lost its barb. The Fear of Death, even among professing Christians, is now comparatively rare; I do not mean merely among dying men—in whom those who have had acquaintance with deathbeds tell us they see it scarcely ever—but with the quick and hale. Even with very ignorant persons, the idea that things may be a great deal worse for us hereafter than even at present is not generally entertained as respects themselves. A clergyman who was attending a sick man in his parish expressed a hope to the wife that she took occasion to remind her husband of his spiritual condition. 'Oh yes, sir,' she replied, 'many and many a time have I woke him up o' nights, and cried, "John, John, you little know the torments as is preparing for you."' But the good woman, it seems, was not disturbed by any such dire imaginings upon her own account.

Higher in the social scale, the apprehension of a Gehenna, or at all events of such a one as our forefathers almost universally believed in, is rapidly dying out. The mathematician tells us that even as a question of numbers, 'about one in ten, my good sir, by the most favourable computations,' the thing is incredible; the philanthropist inquires indignantly, 'Is the city Arab then, who grows to be thief and felon as naturally as a tree puts forth its leaves, to be damned in both worlds?' and I notice that even the clergy who come my way, and take their weak glass of negus while the coach changes horses, no longer insist upon the point, but, at the worst, 'faintly trust the larger hope.'

Notwithstanding these comparatively cheerful views upon a subject so important to all passengers on life's highway, the general feeling is, as I have said, one of profound dissatisfaction; the good old notion that whatever is is right, is fast disappearing; and in its place there is a doubt—rarely expressed except among the philosophers, with whom, as I have said, I have nothing to do—a secret, harassing, and unwelcome doubt respecting the divine government of the world. It is a question which the very philosophers are not likely to settle even among themselves, but it has become very obtrusive and important. Men raise their eyebrows and shrug their shoulders when it is alluded to, instead, as of old, of pulverising the audacious questioner on the spot, or even (as would have happened at a later date) putting him into Coventry; they have no opinion to offer upon the subject, or at all events do not wish to talk about it. But it is no longer, be it observed, 'bad form' in a general way to do so; it is only that the topic is personally distasteful.

The once famous advocate of analogy threw a bitter seed among mankind when he suggested, in all innocence, and merely for the sake of his own argument, that as the innocent suffered for the guilty in this world, so it might be in the world to come; and it is bearing bitter fruit. To feel aweary at the Midway Inn is bad enough; but to be journeying to no home, and perhaps even to some harsher school than we yet wot of, is indeed a depressing reflection.

Hence it comes, I think, or partly hence, that there is now no fun in the world. Wit we have, and an abundance of grim humour, which evokes anything but mirth. Nothing would astonish us in the Midway Inn so much as a peal of laughter. A great writer (though it must be confessed scarcely an amusing one), who has recently reached his journey's end, used to describe his animal spirits depreciatingly, as being at the best but vegetable spirits. And that is now the way with us all. When Charles Dickens died, it was confidently stated in a great literary journal that his loss, so far from affecting 'the gaiety of nations,' would scarcely be felt at all; the power of rousing tears and laughter being (I suppose the writer thought) so very common. That prophecy has been by no means fulfilled. But, what is far worse than there being no humorous writers amongst us, the faculty of appreciating even the old ones is dying out. There is no such thing as high spirits anywhere. It is observable, too, how very much public entertainments have increased of late—a tacit acknowledgment of dulness at home—while, instead of the lively, if somewhat boisterous, talk of our fathers, we have drawing-room dissertations on art, and dandy drivel about blue china.

There is one pleasure only that takes more and more root amongst us, and never seems to fail, and that is making money. To hear the passengers at the Midway Inn discourse upon this topic, you would think they were all commercial travellers. It is most curious how the desire for pecuniary gain has infected even the idlest, who of course take the shortest cut to it by way of the race-course. I see young gentlemen, blond and beardless, telling the darkest secrets to one another, affecting, one would think, the fate of Europe, but which in reality relate to the state of the fetlock of the brother to Boanerges. Their earnestness (which is reserved for this enthralling topic) is quite appalling. In their elders one has long been accustomed to it, but these young people should really know better. The interest excited in society by 'scratchings' has never been equalled since the time of the Cock Lane ghost. If men would only 'lose their money and look pleasant' without talking about it, I shouldn't mind; but they *will* make it a subject of conversation, as though everyone who liked his glass of wine should converse upon 'the vintages.' One looks for it in business people and forgives it; but everyone is now for business.

The reverence that used to belong to Death is now only paid to it in the case of immensely rich persons, whose wealth is spoken of with bated breath. 'He died, sir, worth two millions; a very warm man.' If you happen to say, though with all reasonable probability and even with Holy Writ to back you, 'He is probably warmer by this time,' you are looked upon as a Communist. What the man was is nothing, what he made is everything. It is the gold alone that we now value: the temple that might have sanctified the gold is of no account. This worship of mere wealth has, it is true, this advantage over the old adoration of birth, that something may possibly be got out of it; to cringe and fawn upon the people that have blue blood is manifestly futile, since the peculiarity is not communicable, but it is hoped that, by being shaken up in the same social bag with millionaires, something may be attained by what is technically called the 'sweating' process. So far as I have observed, however, the results are small, while the operation is to the last degree disagreeable.

What is very significant of this new sort of golden age is that a literature of its own has arisen, though of an anomalous kind. It is presided over by a sort of male Miss Kilmansegge, who is also a model of propriety. It is as though the dragon that guarded the apples of Hesperides should be a dragon of virtue. Under the pretence of extolling prudence and perseverance, he paints money-making as the highest good, and calls it thrift; and the popularity of this class of book is enormous. The heroes are all 'self-made' men who come to town with that proverbial half-crown which has the faculty of accumulation that used to be confined to snowballs. Like the daughters of the horse-leech, their cry is 'Give, give,' only instead of blood they want money; and I need hardly say they get it from other people's pockets. Love and friendship are names that have lost their meaning, if they ever had any, with these gentry. They remind one of the miser of old who could not hear a large sum of money mentioned without an acceleration of the action of the heart; and perhaps that is the use of their hearts, which, otherwise, like that of the spleen in other people, must be only a subject of vague conjecture. They live abhorred and die respected; leaving all their heaped-up wealth to some charitable institution, the secretary of which levants with it eventually to the United States.

This last catastrophe, however, is not mentioned in these biographies, the subjects of which are held up as patterns of wisdom and prudence for the rising generation. I shall have left the Midway Inn, thank Heaven, for a residence of smaller dimensions, before it has grown up. Conceive an England inhabited by self-made men!

Has it ever struck you how gloomy is the poetry of the present day? This is not perhaps of very much consequence, since everybody has a great deal too much to do to permit them to read it; but how full of sighs, and groans, and passionate bewailings it is! And also how deuced difficult! It is almost as inarticulate as an Æolian harp, and quite as melancholy. There are one or two exceptions, of course, as in the case of Mr. Calverley and Mr.

Locker; but even the latter is careful to insist upon the fact that, like those who have gone before us, we must all quit Piccadilly. 'At present,' as dear Charles Lamb writes, 'we have the advantage of them;' but there is no one to remind us of that now, nor is it, as I have said, the general opinion that it *is* an advantage.

It is this prevailing gloom, I think, which accounts for the enormous and increasing popularity of fiction. Observe how story-telling creeps into the very newspapers (along with their professional fibbing); and, even in the magazines, how it lies down side by side with 'burning questions,' like the weaned child putting its hand into the cockatrice's den. For your sake, my good fellow, who write stories [here my friend glowered at me compassionately], I am glad of it; but the fact is of melancholy significance. It means that people are glad to find themselves 'anywhere, anywhere, out of the world,' and (I must be allowed to add) they are generally gratified, for anything less like real life than what some novelists portray it is difficult to imagine.

[Here he stared at me so exceedingly hard, that anyone with a less heavenly temper, or who had no material reasons for putting up with it, would have taken his remark as personal, and gone away.

Another cause of the absence of good fellowship amongst us (he went on) is the growth of education. It sticks like a fungus to everybody, and though, it is fair to say, mostly outside, does a great deal of mischief. The scholastic interest has become so powerful that nobody dares speak a word against it; but the fact is, men are educated far beyond their wits. You can't fill any cup beyond what it will hold, and the little cups are exceedingly numerous. Boys are now crammed (with information) like turkeys (but unfortunately not killed at Christmas), and when they grow up there is absolutely no room in them for a joke. The prigs that frequent my Midway Inn are as the sands in its hour-glass, only with no chance, alas! of their running out. The wisdom of our ancestors limited education, and very wisely, to the three R's; that is all that is necessary for the great mass of mankind: whereas the pick of them, with those clamping irons well stuck to their heels, will win their way to the topmost peaks of knowledge.

At the very best—that is to say when it produces *anything*—what does the most costly education in this country produce in ordinary minds but the deplorable habit of classical quotation? If it could teach them to *think*—but that is a subject, my dear friend, into which you will scarcly follow me.

[I could have knocked his head off if he had not been so exceptionally stout and strong, and as it was, I took up my hat to go, when a thought struck me.]

'Among your valuable remarks upon the ideas entertained by society at present, you have said nothing, my dear sir, about the ladies.'

'I never speak of anything,' he replied with dignity, 'which I do not thoroughly understand. Man I do know—down to his boots; but woman'—here he sighed and hesitated—'no; I don't know nearly so much of her.'

THE CRITIC ON THE HEARTH.

It has often struck me that the relation of two important members of the social body to one another has never been sufficiently considered, or treated of, so far as I know, either by the philosopher or the poet. I allude to that which exists between the omnibus driver and his conductor. Cultivating literature as I do upon a little oatmeal, and driving, when in a position to be driven at all, in that humble vehicle, the 'bus, I have had, perhaps, exceptional opportunities for observing their mutual position and behaviour; and it is very peculiar. When the 'bus is empty, these persons are sympathetic and friendly to one another, almost to tenderness; but when there is much traffic, a tone of severity is observable upon the side of the conductor. 'What are yer a-driving on for just as a party's getting in? Will nothing suit but to break a party's neck?' 'Wake up, will yer? or do yer want that ere Bayswater to pass us?' are inquiries he will make in the most peremptory manner. Or he will concentrate contempt in the laconic but withering observation: 'Now then, stoopid!'

When we consider that the driver is after all the driver—that the 'bus is under his guidance and management, and may be said *pro tem*, to be his own—indeed, in case of collision or other serious extremity, he calls it so: 'What the infernal regions are yer banging into my 'bus for?' etc., etc.,—I say, this being his exalted position, the injurious language of the man on the step is, to say the least of it, disrespectful.

On the other hand, it is the conductor who fills the 'bus, and even entices into it, by lures and wiles, persons who are not voluntarily going his way at all. It is he who advertises its presence to the passers-by, and spares neither lung nor limb in attracting passengers. If the driver is lord and king, yet the conductor has a good deal to do with the administration: just as the Mikado of Japan, who sits above the thunder and is almost divine, is understood to be assisted and even 'conducted' by the Tycoon. The connection between those potentates is perhaps the most exact reproduction of that between the 'bus driver and his cad; but even in England there is a pretty close parallel to it in the mutual relation of the author and the professional critic.

While the former is in his spring-time, the analogy is indeed almost complete. For example, however much he may have plagiarised, the book does belong to the author: he calls it, with pardonable pride (and especially if anyone runs it down), 'my book.' He has written it, and probably paid pretty handsomely for getting it published. Even the right of translation, if you will look at the bottom of the title-page, is somewhat superfluously reserved to him. Yet nothing can exceed the patronage which he suffers at the hands of the critic, and is compelled to submit to in sullen silence. When the book-trade is slack—that is, in the summer season—the pair get on together pretty amicably. 'This book,' says the critic, 'may be taken down to the seaside, and lounged over not unprofitably;' or, 'Readers may do worse than peruse this unpretending little volume of fugitive verse;' or even, 'We hail this new aspirant to the laurels of Apollo.' But in the thick of the publishing season, and when books pour into the reviewer by the cartful, nothing can exceed the violence, and indeed sometimes the virulence, of his language. That 'Now then, stoopid!' of the 'bus conductor pales beside the lightnings of his scorn.

'Among the lovers of sensation, it is possible that some persons may be found with tastes so utterly vitiated as to derive pleasure from this monstrous production.' I cull these flowers of speech from a wreath placed by a critic of the *Slasher* on my own early brow. Ye gods, how I hated him! How I pursued him with more than Corsican vengeance; traduced him in public and private; and only when I had thrust my knife (metaphorically) into his detested carcase, discovered I had been attacking the wrong man. It is a lesson I have never forgotten; and I pray you, my younger brothers of the pen, to lay it to heart. Believe rather that your unfriendly critic, like the bee who is fabled to sting and die, has perished after his attempt on your reputation; and let the tomb be his asylum. For even supposing you get the right sow by the ear—or rather, the wild boar with the 'raging tooth'—what can it profit you? It is not like that difference of opinion between yourself and twelve of your fellow-countrymen which may have such fatal results. You are not an Adonis (except in outward form, perhaps), that you can be ripped up with his tusk. His hard words do not break your bones. If they are uncalled for, their cruelty, believe me, can hurt only your vanity. While it is just possible—though indeed in your case in the very highest degree improbable—that the gentleman may have been right.

In the good old times we are told that a buffet from the hand of an Edinburgh or Quarterly Reviewer would lay a young author dead at his feet. If it was so, he must have been naturally very deficient in vitality. It certainly did not kill Byron, though it was a knock-down blow; he rose from that combat from earth, like Antæus, all the stronger for it. The story of its having killed Keats, though embalmed in verse, is apocryphal; and if such blows were not fatal in those times, still less so are they nowadays. On the other hand, if authors are difficult to slay, it is infinitely harder work to give them life by what the doctors term 'artificial respiration'—puffing. The amount of breath expended in the days of 'the Quarterlies' in this hopeless task would have moved windmills. Not a single favourite of those critics—selected, that is, from favouritism, and apart from merit—now survives. They failed even to obtain immortality for the writers in whom there was really something of genius, but whom they extolled beyond their deserts. Their pet idol, for example, was Samuel Rogers. And who reads Rogers's poems now? We remember something about them, and that is all; they are very literally 'Pleasures of Memory.'

And if these things are true of the past, how much more so are they of the present! I venture to think, in spite of some voices to the contrary, that criticism is much more honest than it used to be: certainly less influenced by political feeling, and by the interests of publishing houses; more temperate, if not more judicious, and—in the higher literary organs, at least—unswayed by personal prejudice. But the result of even the most favourable notices upon a book is now but small. I can remember when a review in the *Times* was calculated by the 'Row' to sell an entire edition. Those halcyon days—if halcyon days they were—are over. People read books for themselves now; judge for themselves; and buy only when they are absolutely compelled, and cannot get them from the libraries. In the case of an author who has already secured a public, it is indeed extraordinary what little effect reviews, either good or bad, have upon his circulation. Those who like his works continue to read them, no matter what evil is written of them; and those who don't like them are not to be persuaded (alas!) to change their minds, though his latest effort should be described as though it had dropped from the heavens. I could give some statistics upon this point not a little surprising, but statistics involve comparisons—which are odious. As for fiction, its success depends more upon what Mrs. Brown says to Mrs. Jones as to the necessity of getting that charming book from the library while there is yet time, than on all the reviews in Christendom.

O Fame! if I e'er took delight in thy praises,

'Twas less for the sake of thy high-sounding phrases

Than to see the bright eyes of those dear ones discover

They thought that I was not unworthy—

of a special messenger to Mr. Mudie's.

Heaven bless them! for, when we get old and stupid, they still stick by one, and are not to be seduced from their allegiance by any blaring of trumpets, or clashing of cymbals, that heralds a new arrival among the story-tellers.

On the other hand, as respects his first venture, the author is very dependent upon what the critics say of him. It is the conductor, you know (I wouldn't call him a 'cad,' even in fun, for ten thousand pounds), on whom, to return to our metaphor, the driver is dependent for the patronage of his vehicle, and even for the announcement of its existence. A good review is still the very best of advertisements to a new author; and even a bad one is better than no review at all. Indeed, I have heard it whispered that a review which speaks unfavourably of a work of fiction, upon moral grounds, is of very great use to it. This, however, the same gossips say, is mainly confined to works of fiction written by female authors for readers of their own sex—'*by* ladies *for* ladies,' as a feminine *Pall Mall Gazette* might describe itself.

Nor would I be understood to say that even a well-established author is not affected by what the critics may say of him; I only state that his circulation is not—albeit they may make his very blood curdle. I have a popular writer in my mind, who never looks at a newspaper unless it comes to him by a hand he can trust, for fear his eyes should light upon an unpleasant review. His argument is this: 'I have been at this work for the last twelve months, thinking of little else and putting my best intelligence (which is considerable) at its service. Is it humanly probable that a reviewer who has given his mind to it for a less number of hours, can suggest anything in the way of improvement worthy of my consideration? I am supposing him to be endowed with ability and actuated by good faith; that he has not failed in my own profession and is not jealous of my popularity; yet even thus, how is it possible that his opinion can be of material advantage to me? If favourable, it gives me pleasure, because it flatters my *amour propre*, and I am even not quite sure that it does not afford a stimulating encouragement; but if unfavourable, I own it gives me considerable annoyance. [This is his euphemistic phrase to express the feeling of being in a hornets' nest without his clothes on.] On the other hand, if the critic is a mere hireling, or a young gentleman from the university who is trying his 'prentice hand at a lowish rate of remuneration upon a veteran like myself, how still more idle would it be to regard his views!'

And it appears to me that there is really something in these arguments. As regards the latter part of them, by-the-bye, I had the pleasure of seeing my own last immortal story spoken of in an American magazine—the *Atlantic Monthly*—as the work of 'a bright and prosperous young author.' The critic (Heaven bless his young heart, and give him a happy Whitsuntide) evidently imagined it to be my first production. In another Transatlantic organ, a critic, speaking of the last work of that literary veteran, the late Mr. Le Fanu, observes: 'If this young writer would only model himself upon the works of Mr. William Black in his best days, we foresee a great future before him.'

There is one thing that I think should be set down to the credit of the literary profession—that for the most part they take their 'slatings' (which is the professional term for them) with at least outward equanimity. I have read things of late, written of an old and popular writer, ten times more virulent than anything Mr. Ruskin wrote of Mr. Whistler: yet neither he, nor any other man of letters, thinks of flying to his mother's apron-string, or of setting in motion old Father Antic, the Law. Perhaps it is that we have no money, or perhaps, like the judicious author of whom I have spoken, we abstain from reading unpleasant things. I wish to goodness we could abstain from hearing of them; but the 'd——d good-natured friend' is an eternal creation. He has altered, however, since Sheridan's time in his method of proceeding. He does not say, 'There is a very unpleasant notice of you in the *Scorpion*, my dear fellow, which I deplore.' The scoundrel now affects a more light-hearted style. 'There is a review of your last book in the *Scorpion*', he says, 'which will amuse you. It is very malicious, and evidently the offspring of personal spite, but it is very clever.' Then you go down to your club, and take the thing up with the tongs, when nobody is looking, and make yourself very miserable; or you buy it, going home in the cab, and, having spoilt your appetite for dinner with it, tear it up very small, throw it out of window, and swear you have never seen it.

One forgives the critic—perhaps—but never the good-natured friend. It is always possible—to the wise man—to refrain from reading the lucubration of the former, but he cannot avoid the latter: which brings me to the main subject of this paper—the Critic on the Hearth. One can be deaf to the voice of the public hireling, but it is impossible to shut one's ears to the private communications of one's friends and family—all meant for our good, no doubt, but which are nevertheless insufferable.

In Miss Martineau's Autobiography there is a passage expressing her surprise that whereas in all other cases there is a certain modest reticence in respect to other people's business when it is of a special kind, the profession of literature is made an exception. As there is no one but imagines that he can poke a fire and drive a gig, so everyone believes he can write a book, or at all events (like that blasphemous person in connection with the Creation) that he can give a wrinkle or two to the author.

I wonder what a parson would say, if a man who never goes to church save when his babies are christened, or by accident to get out of a shower, should volunteer his advice about sermon-making? or an artist, to whom the man without arms, who is wheeled about in the streets for coppers, should recommend a greater delicacy of touch? Indeed, metaphor fails me, and I gasp for mere breath when I think of the astounding impudence of some people. If I possessed a tithe of it, I should surely have made my fortune by this time, and be in the enjoyment of the greatest prosperity. It must be remembered, too, that the opinion of the Critics on the Hearth is always volunteered (indeed, one would as soon think of asking for it as for a loan from the Sultan of Turkey), and in nine cases out of ten it is unfavourable. One has no objection to their praise, nor to any amount of it; what is so abhorrent is their advice, and still more their disapproval. It is like throwing 'half a brick' at you, which, utterly valueless in itself, still hurts you when it hits you. And the worst of it is that, apart from their rubbishy opinions, one likes these people; they are one's friends and relatives, and to cut one's moorings from them altogether would be to sail over the sea of life without a port to touch at.

The early life of the author is especially embittered by the utterances of these good folks. As a prophet is of no honour in his own country, so it is with the young aspirant for literary fame with his folks at home. They not only disbelieve in him, but—generally, however, with one or two exceptions, who are invaluable to him in the way of encouragement—'make hay' of him and his pretensions in the most heartless style. If he produces a poem, it achieves immortality in the sense of his 'never hearing the last of it;' it is the jest of the family till they have all grown up. But this he can bear, because his noble mind recognises its own greatness; he regards his jeering brethren in the same light as the philosophic writer beholds 'the vapid and irreflective reader.' When they tell him they 'can't make head or tail of his blessed poetry,' he comforts himself with the reflection of the great German (which he has read in a translation) that the clearest handwriting cannot be read by twilight. It is when his literary talents have received more or less recognition from the public at large, that home criticism becomes so painful to him. His brethren are then boys no longer, but parsons, lawyers, and doctors; and though they don't venture to interfere with one-another as regards their individual professions, they make no sort of scruple about interfering with *him*. They write to him their unsolicited advice and strictures. This is the parson's letter:

'MY DEAR DICK, 'I like your last book much better than the rest of them; but I don't like your heroine. She strikes both Julia and myself [Julia is his wife, who is acquainted with no literature but the cookery-book] as rather namby-pamby. The descriptions, however, are charming; we both recognised dear old Ramsgate at once. [The original of the locality in the novel being Dieppe.] The plot is also excellent, though we think we have some recollection of it elsewhere; but it must be so difficult to hit upon anything original in these days. Thanks for your kind remembrance of us at

Christmas: the oysters were excellent. We were sorry to see that ill-natured little notice in the *Scourge*.

'Yours affectionately,
'BOB.'

Jack the lawyer writes:

'DEAR DICK, 'You are really becoming ["Becoming?" he thinks *that* becoming] quite a great man: we could hardly get your last book from Mudie's, though I suppose he takes very small quantities of copies, except from really popular authors. Marion was charmed with your heroine [Dick rather likes Marion; and doesn't think Jack treats her with the consideration she deserves], and I have no doubt women in general will admire her, but your hero—you know I always speak my mind—is rather a duffer. You should go into the world more, and sketch from life. The Vice-Chancellor gave me great pleasure by speaking of your early poems very highly the other day, and I assure you it was quite a drop down for me, to find that he was referring to some other writer of the same name. Of course I did not undeceive him. I wish, my dear fellow, you would write stories in one volume instead of three. You write a *short* story capitally.

'Yours ever,
'JACK.'

Tom the surgeon belongs to that very objectionable class of humanity, called, by ancient writers, wags:

'MY DEAR DICK, 'I cannot help writing to thank you for the relief afforded to me by the perusal of your last volume. I had been suffering from neuralgia, and every prescription in the Pharmacopæia for producing sleep had failed until I tried *that*. Dear Maggie [an odious woman, who calls novels "light literature," and affects to be blue] read it to me herself, so it was given every chance; but I think you must acknowledge that it was a little spun out. Maggie assures me—I have not read them myself, for you know what little time I have for such things—that the first two volumes, with the exception of the characters of the hero and heroine, which she pronounces to be rather feeble, are first-rate. Why don't you write two-volume novels? There is always something in analogy: reflect how seldom Nature herself produces three at a birth: when she does, it is only two, at most, which survive. We shall look forward to your next effort with much interest, but we hope you will give more time and pains to it. Remember what Horace says upon this subject (He has no more knowledge of Horace than he has of Sanscrit, but he has read the quotation in that vile review in the *Scourge*.) Maggie thinks you live too luxuriously: if your expenses were less you would not be compelled to write so much, and you would do it better. Excuse this well-meant advice from an elder brother.

'Yours always,
'Tom.'

'One's sisters, and one's cousins, and one's aunts' also write in more or less the same style, though, to do their sex justice, less offensively. 'If you were to go abroad, my dear Dick,' says one, 'it would expand your mind. There is nothing to blame in your last production, which strikes me (what I could understand of it at least, for some of it is a little Bohemian) as very pleasing; but the fact is, that English subjects are quite used up.' Others discover for themselves the originals of Dick's characters in persons he has never dreamt of describing, and otherwise exhibit a most marvellous familiarity with his materials. 'Hennie, who has just been here, is immensely delighted with your satirical sketch of her husband. He, however, as you may suppose, is *wild*, and says you had better withdraw your name from the candidates' book at his club. I don't know how many black balls exclude, but he has a good many friends there.' Another writes: 'Of course we all recognised Uncle George in your Mr. Flibbertigibbet; but we try not to laugh; indeed our sense of loss is too recent. Seriously, I think you might have waited till the poor old man—who was always kind to you, Dick—was cold in his grave.'

Some of these excellent creatures send incidents of real life which they are sure will be useful to 'dear Dick' for his next book—narratives of accidents in a hansom cab, of missing the train by the Underground, and of Mr. Jones being late for his own wedding, 'which, though nothing in themselves, actually did happen, you know, and which, properly dressed up, as you so well know how to do,' will, they are sure, obtain for him a marked success. 'There is nothing like reality,' they say, he may depend upon it, 'for coming home to people.'

After all, one need not read these abominable letters. One's relatives (thank Heaven!) usually live in the country. The real Critics on the Hearth are one's personal acquaintances in town, whom one cannot escape.

'My dear friend,' said one to me the other day—a most cordial and excellent fellow, by-the-bye (only too frank)—'I like you, as you know, beyond everything, personally, but I cannot read your books.'

'My dear Jones,' replied I, 'I regret that exceedingly; for it is you, and men like you, whose suffrages I am most anxious to win. Of the approbation of all intelligent and educated persons I am certain; but if I could only obtain that of the million, I should be a happy man.'

But even when I have thus demolished Jones, I still feel that I owe him a grudge. 'What the Deuce is it to me whether Jones likes my books or not? and why does he tell me he doesn't like them?'

Of the surpassing ignorance of these good people, I have just heard an admirable anecdote. A friend of a justly popular author meets him in the club and congratulates him upon his last story in the *Slasher* [in which he has never written a line]. It is so full of farce and fun [the author is a grave writer]. 'Only I don't see why it is not advertised under the same title in the other newspapers.' The fact being that the story in the *Slasher* is a parody—and not a very good-natured one—upon the author's last work, and resembles it only as a picture in *Vanity Fair* resembles its original.

Some Critics on the Hearth are not only good-natured, but have rather too high, or, if that is impossible, let us say too pronounced, an opinion of the abilities of their literary friends. They wonder why they do not employ their gigantic talents in some enduring monument, such as a life of 'Alexander the Great' or a popular history of the Visigoths. To them literature is literature, and they do not concern themselves with little niceties of style or differences of subject. Others again, though extremely civil, are apt to affect more enthusiasm than they feel. They admire one's works without exception—'they are all absolutely charming'—but they would be placed in a position of great embarrassment if they were asked to name their favourite: for, as a matter of fact, they are ignorant of the very names of them. A novelist of my acquaintance lent his last work to a lady cousin because she 'really could not wait till she got it from the library;' besides, 'she was ill, and wanted some amusing literature.' After a month or so he got his three volumes back, with a most gushing letter. It 'had been the comfort of many a weary hour of sleeplessness,' etc. The thought of having 'smoothed the pillow and soothed the pain' would, she felt sure, be gratifying to him. Perhaps it would have been, only she had omitted to cut the pages even of the first volume.

But, as a general rule, these volunteer censors plume themselves on discovering defects and not beauties. When any author is particularly popular and has been long before the public, they have two methods of discoursing upon him in relation to their literary friend. In the first, they represent him as a model of excellence, and recommend their friend to study him, though without holding out much hope of his ever becoming his rival; in the second, they describe him as 'worked out,' and darkly hint that sooner or later [they mean sooner] their friend will be in the same unhappy condition. These, I need not say, are among the most detestable specimens of their class, and only to be equalled by those excellent literary judges who are always appealing to posterity, which, even if a little temporary success has crowned you to-day, will relegate you to your proper position to-morrow. If one were weak enough to argue with these gentry, it would be easy to show that popular authors are not 'worked out,' but only have the appearance of being so from their taking their work too easily. Those whose calling it is to depict human nature in fiction are especially subject to this weakness; they do not give themselves the trouble to study new characters, or at first hand, as of old; they sit at home and receive the congratulations of Society without paying due attention to that somewhat changeful lady, and they draw upon their memory, or their imagination, instead of studying from the life. Otherwise, when they do not give way to that temptation of indolence which arises from competence and success, there is no reason why their reputation should suffer, since, though they may lack the vigour or high spirits of those who would push them from their stools, their experience and knowledge of the world are always on the increase.

As to the argument with regard to posterity which is so popular with the Critic on the Hearth, I am afraid he has no greater respect for the opinion of posterity himself than for that of his possible great-great-granddaughter. Indeed, he only uses it as being a weapon the blow of which it is impossible to parry, and with the object of being personally offensive. It is, moreover, noteworthy that his position, which is sometimes taken up by persons of far greater intelligence, is inconsistent with itself. The praisers of posterity are also always the praisers of the past; it is only the present which is in their eyes contemptible. Yet to the next generation this present will be *their* past, and, however valueless may be the verdict of today, how much more so, by the most obvious analogy, will be that of to-morrow. It is probable, indeed, though it is difficult to believe it, that the Critics on the Hearth of the generation to come will make themselves even more ridiculous than their immediate predecessors.

SHAM ADMIRATION IN LITERATURE.

In all highly civilised communities Pretence is prominent, and sooner or later invades the regions of Literature. In the beginning, this is not altogether to be reprobated; it is the rude homage which Ignorance, conscious of its disgrace, offers to Learning; but after awhile, Pretence becomes systematised, gathers strength from numbers and impunity, and rears its head in such a manner as to suggest it has some body and substance belonging to it. In England, literary pretence is more universal than elsewhere from our method of education. When young gentlemen from ten to sixteen are set to study poetry (a subject for which not one in a hundred has the least taste or capability even when he reads it in his own language) in Greek and Latin authors, it is only a natural consequence that their views upon it should be slightly artificial. The youth who objected to the alphabet that it seemed hardly worth while to have gone through so much to have acquired so little, was exceptionally sagacious; the more ordinary lad conceives that what has cost him so much time and trouble, and entailed so many pains and penalties, must needs have something in it, though it has never met his eye. Hence arises our public opinion upon the ancient classics, which I am afraid is somewhat different from (what painters term) the private view. If you take the ordinary admirer of Æschylus, for example—not the scholar, but the man who has had what he believes to be 'a liberal education'—and appeal to his opinion upon some passage in a British dramatist, say Shakespeare, it is ten to one that he shows not only ignorance of the author (the odds are twenty to one about *that*), but utter inability to grasp the point in question; it is too deep for him, and, especially, too subtle. If you are cruel enough to press him, he will unconsciously betray the fact that he has never felt a line of poetry in his life. He honestly believes that the 'Seven against Thebes' is one of the greatest works that ever were written, just as a child believes the same of the 'Seven Champions of Christendom.' A great wit once observed, when bored by the praises of a man who spoke six languages, that he had known a man to speak a dozen, and yet not say a word worth hearing in any one of them. The humour of the remark, as sometimes happens, has caused its wisdom to be underrated; for the fact is that, in very many cases, all the intelligence of which a mind is capable is expended upon the mere acquisition of a foreign tongue. As to getting anything out of it in the way of ideas, and especially of poetical ones, that is almost never attained. There are, indeed, many who have a special facility for languages, but in their case (with a few exceptions) one may say without uncharity that the acquisition of ideas is not their object, though if they did acquire them they would probably be new ones. The majority of us, however, have much difficulty in surmounting the obstacle of an alien tongue; and when we have done so we are naturally inclined to overrate the advantages thus attained. Everyone knows the poor creature who quotes French on all occasions with a certain stress on the accent, designed to arouse a doubt in his hearers as to whether he was not actually born in Paris. *He*, of course, is a low specimen of the class in question, but almost all of us derive a certain intellectual gratification from the mastery of another language, and as we gradually attain to it, whenever we find a meaning we are apt to mistake it for a beauty.[1] Nay, I am convinced that many admire this or that (even) British poet from the fact that here and there his meaning has gleamed upon them with all the charm that accompanies unexpectedness.

[1] Since the above was written, my attention has been called to the following remark of De Quincey: 'As must ever be the case with readers not sufficiently masters of a language to bring the true pretensions of a work to any test of feeling, they are for ever mistaking for some pleasure conferred by the writer, what is, in fact, the pleasure naturally attached to the sense of a difficulty overcome.'

Since classical learning is compulsory with us, this bastard admiration is much more often excited with respect to the Greek and Latin poets. Men may not only go through the whole curriculum of a university education, but take high honours in it, without the least intellectual advantage beyond the acquisition of a few quotations. This is not, of course (good heavens!), because the classics have nothing to teach us in the way of poetical ideas, but simply because to the ordinary mind the acquisition of a poetical idea is very difficult, and when conveyed in a foreign language is impossible. If the same student had given the same time—a monstrous thought, of course, but not impracticable—to the cultivation of Shakespeare and the old dramatists, or even to the more modern English poets and thinkers, he would certainly have got more out of them, though he would have missed the delicate suggestiveness of the Greek aorist, and the exquisite subtleties of the particle *de*. Having acquired these last, however, and not for nothing, it is not surprising that he should esteem them very highly, and, being unable to popularise them at dinner-parties and the like, he falls back upon praise of the classics generally.

Such are the circumstances which, more particularly in this country, have led to a well-nigh universal habit of literary lying—of a pretence of admiration for certain works of which in reality we know very little, and for which, if we knew more, we should perhaps care even less.

There are certain books which are standard, and as it were planted in the British soil, before which the great majority of us bow the knee and doff the cap with a reverence that, in its ignorance, reminds one of fetish worship, and, in its affectation, of the passion for High Art. The works without which, we are told at book auctions, 'no gentleman's library can be considered complete,' are especially the objects of this adoration. The 'Rambler,' for example, is one of them. I was once shut up for a week of snowstorms in a mountain inn, with the 'Rambler' and one other publication. The latter was a Shepherd's Guide, with illustrations of the way in which sheep are marked by their various owners for the purpose of identification: 'Cropped near ear, upper key bitted far, a pop on the head and another at the tail head, ritted, and with two red strokes down both shoulders,' etc. It was monotonous, but I confess that there were times when I felt it some comfort in having that picture-book to fall back upon, to alternate with the 'Rambler.'

The essay, like port wine, I have noticed, requires age for its due appreciation. Leigh Hunt's 'Indicator' comprises some admirable essays, but the general public have not a word to say for them; it may be urged that that is because they had not read the 'Indicator' But why then do they praise the 'Rambler' and Montaigne? That comforting word, 'Mesopotamia,' which has been so often alluded to in religious matters, has many a parallel in profane literature.

A good deal of this mock worship is of course due to abject cowardice. A man who says he doesn't like the 'Rambler,' runs, with some folks, the risk of being thought a fool; but he is sure to be thought that, for something or another, under any circumstances; and, at all events, why should he not content himself, when the 'Rambler' is belauded, with holding his tongue and smiling acquiescence? It must be conceded that there are a few persons who really have read the 'Rambler,' a work, of course, I am merely using as a type of its class. In their young days it was used as a schoolbook, and thought necessary as a part of polite education; and as they have read little or nothing since, it is only reasonable that they should stick to their colours. Indeed, the French satirist's boast that he could predicate the views of any man with regard to both worlds, if he were only supplied with the simple data of his age and his income, is quite true in the general with regard to literary taste. Given the age of the ordinary individual—that is to say of the gentleman 'fond of books, but who has really no time for reading'—and it is easy enough to guess his literary idols. They are the gods of his youth, and, whether he has been 'suckled in a creed outworn' or not, he knows no other. These persons, however, rarely give their opinion about literary matters, except on compulsion; they are harmless and truthful. The tendency of society in general, on the other hand, is not only to praise the 'Rambler' which they have not read, but to express a noble scorn for those who have read it and don't like it.

I remember, as a young man, being greatly struck by the independence of character exhibited by Miss Bronte in a certain confession she made in respect to Miss Austen's novels. It was at a period when everybody professed to adore them, and especially the great-guns of literature. Walter Scott thought more highly of the genius of the author of 'Mansfield Park' even than of that of his favourite, Miss Edgeworth. Macaulay speaks of her as though she were the Eclipse of novelists—'first, and the rest nowhere'—though his opinion, it is true, lost something of its force from the contempt he expressed for 'the rest,' among whom were some much better ones. Dr. Whewell, a very different type of mind, had 'Mansfield Park,' I believe, read to him on his death-bed. And, indeed, up to the present date, some highly-cultured persons of my acquaintance take the same view. They may be very possibly right, but that is no reason why the people who have never read Miss Austen's novels—and very few have—should ape the fashion. Now, the authoress of 'Jane Eyre' did not derive much pleasure from the perusal of the works of the other Jane. 'I know it's very wrong,' she modestly said, 'but the fact is I can't read them. They have not got story enough in them to engage my attention. I don't want my blood curdled, but I like it stirred. Miss Austen strikes me as milk-and-watery, and, to say truth, as dull.'

This opinion she has, in effect, repeated in her published writings, but I had only heard her verbal expression of it; and I admired her courage. If she had been a man, struggling, as she then was, for a position in literature, she would not have dared to say half as much. For, what is very curious, the advocates of the classic authors—those I mean whom antiquity has more or less hallowed—instead of pitying those unhappy wights who confess their want of appreciation of them, fly at them with bludgeons, and dance upon their prostrate bodies with clogs.

'For who would rush on a benighted man,

And give him two black eyes for being blind?'

inquires the poet. I answer, 'lots of people,' and especially those who worship the pagan divinities of literature. The same thing happens—but *their* fury is more excusable, because they have less natural intelligence—with the lovers of music. Instead of being sorry for the poor folks who have 'no ear,' and whom 'a little music in the evening' bores to extremity, they overwhelm them with reproaches for what is in fact a natural infirmity. 'You Goth! you Vandal!' they exclaim, 'how contemptible is the creature who has no music in his soul!' Which is really very rude. Even persons who are not musical have their feelings. 'Hath not a Jew ears?'—

that is to say, though they have 'no ear,' they understand what is abusive language and resent it.

I am not saying one word against established reputations in literature. The very fact of their being established (even the 'Rambler,' for example, has its merits) is in their favour; and, indeed, some of the works I shall refer to are masterpieces. My objection is to the sham admiration of them, which does their authors no good (for their circulation is now of no consequence to them), and is injurious not only to modern writers (who are generally made the subject of base comparison), but especially to the utterers of this false coin themselves. One cannot tell falsehoods, even about one's views in literature, without injury to one's morals, yet to 'tell the truth and shame the devil' is easy, as it would seem, compared with telling the truth and defying the critics.

I have alluded to the intrepidity of Miss Bronte in this matter; and, curiously enough, it is women who have the most courage in the expression of their literary opinions. It may be said, of course, that this is due to the audacity of ignorance, and a well-known line may be quoted (for some people, as I have said, are rude) in which certain angels (who are *not* women) are represented as being afraid to tread in certain places. But I am speaking of women who are great readers. Miss Martineau once confessed to me that she could see no beauties in 'Tom Jones.' 'Of course,' she said, 'the coarseness disgusts me, but apart from that, I see no sort of merit in it.' 'What?' I replied, 'no humour, no knowledge of human life?' 'No; to me it is a wearisome book.'

I disagreed with her very much upon that point, and do so still; yet, apart from the coarseness (which does not disgust everybody, let me tell you), there is a good deal of tedious reading in 'Tom Jones.' At all events that expression of opinion from such lips strikes me as noteworthy.

It may here be said that there are many English authors of old date, some of whose beauties are unintelligible except to those who are acquainted with the classics; and 'Tom Jones' is one of them. Many of the introductions to the chapters, not to mention a certain travestie of an Homeric battle, must needs be as wearisome to those who are not scholars, as the spectacle of a burlesque is to those who have not seen the original play. This is still more the case with our old poets, especially Milton. I very much doubt, in spite of the universal chorus to the contrary, whether 'Lycidas' is much admired by readers who are only acquainted with English literature; I am quite sure it never touched their hearts as, for example, 'In Memoriam' does.

I once beheld a young lady of great literary taste, and of exquisite sensibility, torn to pieces (figuratively) and trampled upon by a great scholar for venturing to make a comparison between those two poems. Its invocation to the Muses, and the general classical air which pervades it, had destroyed for her the pathos of 'Lycidas,' whereas to her antagonist those very imperfections appeared to enhance its beauty. I did not interfere, because the wretch was her husband, and it would have been worse for her if I had, but my sympathies were entirely with her. Her sad fate—for the massacre took place in public—would, I was well aware, have the effect of making people lie worse than ever about Milton. On that same evening, while some folks were talking about Mr. Morris's 'Earthly Paradise,' I heard a scornful voice exclaim, 'Oh! give ME "Paradise Lost,"' and with that gentleman I *did* have it out. I promptly subjected him to cross-examination, and drove him to that extremity that he was compelled to admit he had never read a word of Milton for forty years, and even then only in extracts from 'Enfield's Speaker.'

With Shakespeare—though there is a good deal of lying about *him*—the case is different, and especially with elderly people; for 'in their day,' as they pathetically term it, Shakespeare was played everywhere, and everyone went to the play. They do not read him, but they recollect him; they are well acquainted with his beauties—that is, with the better known of them—and can quote him with manifest appreciation. They are, intellectually, in a position much superior to that of a fashionable lady of my acquaintance who informed me that her daughters were going to the theatre that night to see Shakespeare's 'Turning of the Screw.'

The writer who has done most, without I suppose intending it, to promote hypocrisy in literature is Macaulay. His 'every schoolboy knows' has frightened thousands into pretending to know authors with whom they have not even a bowing acquaintance. It is amazing that a man who had read so much should have written so contemptuously of those who have read but little; one would have thought that the consciousness of superiority would have forbidden such insolence, or that his reading would have been extensive enough to teach him at least how little he had read of what there was to read; since he read some things—works of imagination and humour, for example—to such very little purpose, he might really have bragged a little less. One feels quite grateful to Macaulay, however, for avowing his belief that he was the only man who had read through the 'Faery Queen;' since that exonerates everybody—I do not say from reading it, because the supposition is preposterous—but from the necessity of pretending to have read it. The pleasure derived from that poem to most minds is, I am convinced, analogous to that already spoken of as being imparted by a foreign author: namely, the satisfaction at finding it—in places—intelligible. For the few who possess the poetic faculty it has great beauties, but I observe, from the extracts that appear in Poetic Selections and the like, that the most tedious and even the most monstrous passages are those which are generally offered for admiration. The case of Spenser in this respect—which does not stand alone in ancient English literature—has a curious parallel in art, where people are positively found to go into ecstasies over a distorted limb or a ludicrous inversion of perspective, simply because it is the work of an old master, who knew no better, or followed the fashion of his time.

Leigh Hunt read the 'Faery Queen,' by-the-bye, as almost everything else that has been written in the English tongue, and even Macaulay alludes with rare commendation to his 'catholic taste.' Of all authors indeed, and probably of all readers, Leigh Hunt had the keenest eye for merit and the warmest appreciation of it wherever found. He was actively engaged in politics, yet was never blind to the genius of an adversary; blameless himself in morals, he could admire the wit of Wycherley; and a freethinker in religion, he could see both wisdom and beauty in the divines. Moreover, it is immensely to his credit that this universal knowledge, instead of puffing him up, only moved him to impart it, and that next to the pleasure he took in books was that he derived from teaching others to take pleasure in them. Witness his 'Wit and Humour' and his 'Imagination and Fancy,' to my mind the greatest treasures in the way of handbooks that have ever been offered to students of English literature, and the completest antidotes to pretence in it. How many a time, as a boy, have I pondered over this or that passage in the originals, from Shakespeare to Suckling, and then compared it with the italicised lines in his two volumes, to see whether I had hit upon the beauties; and how often, alas! I hit upon the blots![2]

[2] I remember (when 'I was but a little tiny boy') I thought that 'the fringed curtains of thine eye advance,' addressed by Prospero to Miranda, must needs be a very fine line; imagine then my confusion, on referring for corroboration to my 'guide, philosopher, and friend,' as he truly was, to find this passage: 'Why Shakespeare should have condescended to the elaborate nothingness, not to say nonsense, of this metaphor (for what is meant by "advancing curtains"?) I cannot conceive. That is to say, if he did condescend: for it looks very like the interpolation of some pompous declamatory player. Pope has put it into his *Treatise on the Bathos*.'

It is curious that Leigh Hunt, whose style has been so severely handled (and, it must be owned, not without some justice) for its affectations, should have been so genuine (although always generous) in his criticisms. It was nothing to him whether an author was old or new; nor did he shrink from any literary comparison between two writers when he thought it appropriate (and he was generally right), notwithstanding all the age and authority that might be at the back of one of them. Thackeray, by the way, a very different writer and thinker, had this same outspoken honesty in the expression of his literary taste. In speaking of the hero of Cooper's five good novels—Leather-Stocking, Hawkeye, etc.—he remarks with quite a noble simplicity: 'I think he is better than any of Scott's lot.'

It is a 'far cry' from the 'Faery Queen' to 'Childe Harold,' which, reckoning by years, is still a modern poem; yet I wonder how many persons under thirty—even of those who term it 'magnificent'—have ever read 'Childe Harold.' At one time it was only people under thirty who *had* read it; for poetry to the ordinary reader is the poetry that was popular in his youth—'no other is genuine.'

'A dreary, weary poem called the *Excursion*,

Written in a manner which is my aversion,'

is a couplet the frankness of which has always recommended itself to me (though I like the 'Excursion'); but, except for the rhyme, it has a fatal facility of application to other long poems. Heaven forbid that I should 'with shadowed hint confuse' the faith in a British classic; but, ye gods, how men have gaped (in private) over 'Childe Harold!'

'Gil Blas,' though not a native classic, is included in the articles of the British literary faith; not as a matter of pious opinion, but *de fide*; a necessity of intellectual salvation. I remember an interview I once had with a boy of letters concerning this immortal work; he is a well-known writer now, but at the time I speak of he was only budding and sprouting in the magazines—a lad of promise, no doubt, but given, if not to kick against authority, to question it, and, what was worse, to question *me* about it, in an embarrassing manner. The natural affability of my disposition had caused him, I suppose, to treat me as his Father Confessor in literature; and one of the sins of omission he confided to me was in connection with the divine Le Sage.

'I say—about "Gil Blas," you know—Bias [a great critic of that day] was saying last night that if he were to be imprisoned for life with only one book to read he would choose the Bible or "Gil Blas."'

'It is very gratifying to me,' said I, wishing to evade my young friend, and also because I had no love for Bias, 'that he should have selected the Bible, even as an alternative; and all the more so, since I should never have expected it of him.'

'Yes, papa' (that was what the young dog was wont to call me, though he was no son of mine—far from it); 'but about "Gil Blas"? Is it *really* the next best book? And after he had read it—say ten times—would he not have been rather sorry that he had not chosen—well, Shakespeare, for instance?'

The picture of Bias with a long white beard, the growth of twenty years, reading that tattered copy of 'Gil Blas' in his cell, almost affected me to tears; but I made shift to answer gravely: 'Bias is a professional critic; and persons of that class are apt to be a little dogmatic and given to exaggeration. But "Gil Blas" is a great work. As a picture of the seamy side of human life—of its vices and its weaknesses at least—it is unrivalled. The archbishop——'

'Oh! I know that archbishop—*well*,' interrupted my young tormentor. 'I sometimes think, if it hadn't been for that archbishop, we should never perhaps have heard of "Gil Blas."'

'Tchut, tchut!' said I; 'you talk like a child.'

'But to read it *all through*, papa—three times, ten times, for all one's life? Poor Mr. Bias!'

'It is a matter of opinion, my dear boy,' I said. 'Bias has this great advantage over you in literary matters, that he knows what he is talking about; and if he was quite sure——'

'Oh! but he was not quite sure: he was rather doubtful, he said, about one of the books.'

'Not the Bible, I do hope?' said I fervently.

'No, about the other. He was not quite sure but that, instead of "Gil Blas," he ought to have selected "Don Quixote." Now really that seems to me worse than "Gil Blas."'

'You mean less excellent,' I rejoined; 'you are too young to appreciate the full signification of "Don Quixote."'

The scoundrel murmured, 'Do you mean to tell me people read it when they are old?' But I pretended not to hear him. 'We do not all of us,' I went on, 'know what is good for us. Sancho Panza's physician——'

'Oh! I know that physician—*well*, papa. I sometimes think, if it had not been for that physician, perhaps——'

'Hush!' I exclaimed authoritatively; 'let us have no flippancy, I beg.' And so, with a dead lift as it were, I got rid of him. He left the room muttering, 'But to read it through—three times, ten times, for all one's life?' And I was obliged to confess to myself that such a prolonged course of study, even of 'Don Quixote,' would have been wearisome.

Rabelais is another article of our literary faith, that is certainly subscribed to much more often than believed in. In a certain poem of Mr. Browning's (*I* call it the Burial of the Book, since the Latin name he has given it is unpronounceable, even if it were possible to recollect it), charmingly humorous, and which is also remarkable for impersonating an inanimate object in verse as Dickens does in prose, there occur these lines:

'Then I went indoors, brought out a loaf,

Half a cheese and a bottle of Chablis,

Lay on the grass, and forgot the oaf

Over a jolly chapter of Rabelais.'

Yet I have known some wonder to be expressed (confidentially) as to where he found the 'jolly chapter,' and the looking for the beauties of Rabelais to be likened to searching in a huge dung-heap for a few heads of asparagus.

I have no quarrel with Bias and Company (though they stick at nothing, and will presently say that I don't care for these books myself), but I venture to think that they are wrong in making dogmas of what are, after all, but matters of literary taste; it is their vehemence and exaggeration which drive the weak to take refuge in falsehood.

A good woman in the country once complained of her stepson, 'He will not love his learning, though I beats him with a jack-chain;' and from the application of similar aids to instruction, the same result takes place in London. Only here we dissemble and pretend to love it. It is partly in consequence of this that works, not only of acknowledged but genuine excellence, such as those I have been careful to select, are, though so universally praised, so little read. The poor student attempts them, but failing—from many causes no doubt, but also sometimes from the fact of their not being there—to find those unrivalled beauties which he has been led to expect in every sentence, he stops short, where he would otherwise have gone on. He says to himself, 'I have been deceived,' or 'I must be a born fool;' whereas he is wrong in both suppositions. I am convinced that the want of popularity of Walter Scott among the rising generation is partly due to this extravagant laudation; and I am much mistaken if another great author, more recently deceased, will not in a few years be added to the ranks of those who are more praised than read from the same cause.

The habit of mere adhesion to received opinion in any matter is most mischievous, for it strikes at the root of independence of thought; and in literature it tends to make the public taste mechanical. It is very seldom that what is called the verdict of posterity (absurdly enough, for are not *we* posterity?) is ever reversed; but it has chanced to happen in a certain case quite lately. The production of 'The Iron Chest' upon the stage has once more brought into fashion 'Caleb Williams.' Now that is a work, though by no means belonging to the same rank as those to which I have referred, which has a fine old crusted reputation. Time has hallowed it. The great world of readers (who have never read it) used to echo the remark of Bias and Company, that this and that modern work of fiction reminded them—though at an immense distance, of course—of Godwin's masterpiece. I remember Le Fanu's 'Uncle Silas,' for example (from some similarity, more fanciful perhaps than real, in the isolation of its hero), being thus compared with it. Now 'Caleb Williams' is founded on a very fine conception—one that could only have occurred, perhaps, to a man of genius; the first part of it is well worked out, but towards the middle it grows feeble, and it ends in tediousness and drivel; whereas 'Uncle Silas' is good and strong from first to last. Le Fanu has never been so popular as, in my humble judgment, he deserves to be, but of course modern readers were better acquainted with him than with Godwin. Yet nine out of ten were always heard repeating this cuckoo cry about the latter's superiority, until the 'Iron Chest' came out, and Fashion induced them to read Godwin for themselves; which has very properly changed their opinion.

I remember, in my own case, that, from that reverence for authority which I hope I share with my neighbours, I used to speak of 'Headlong Hall' and 'Crotchet Castle'—both great favourites of our fore-fathers—with much respect, until one wet day in the country I found myself shut up with them. I won't say what I suffered; better judges of literature than myself admire them still, I know. I will only remark that *I* don't admire them. I don't say they are the dullest novels ever printed, because that would be invidious, and might do wrong to works of even greater pretensions; but to my mind they are dull.

When Dr. Johnson is free to confess that he does not admire Gray's 'Elegy,' and Macaulay to avow that he sees little to praise in Dickens and Wordsworth, why should not humbler folks have the courage of their own opinions? They cannot possibly be more wrong than Johnson and Macaulay were, and it is surely better to be honest, though it may expose one to some ridicule, than to lie. The more we agree with the verdict of the generations before us on these matters, the more, it is quite true, we are likely to be right; but the agreement should be an honest one. At present very extensive domains in literature are, as it were, enclosed and denied to the public in respect to any free expression of their opinion. 'They are splendid, they are faultless,' cries the general voice, but the general eye has not beheld them. Nothing, of course, could be more futile than that, with every new generation, our old authors who have won their fame should be arraigned anew at the bar of public criticism; but, on the other hand, there is no reason why the mouths of us poor moderns should be muzzled, and still less that we 'should praise with alien lips.'

'Until Caldecott's charming illustrations of it made me laugh so much,' said a young lady to me the other day, 'I confess—though I know it's very stupid of me—I never saw much fun in "John Gilpin."' She evidently expected a reproof, and when I whispered in her ear, 'Nor I,' her lovely features assumed a look of positive enfranchisement.

'But am I right?' she inquired.

'You are certainly right, my dear young lady,' said I, 'not to pretend admiration where you don't feel it; as to liking "John Gilpin," that is a matter of taste. It has, of course, simplicity to recommend it; but in my own case, though I'm fond of fun, it has never evoked a smile. It has always seemed to me like one of Mr. Joe Miller's stories put into tedious verse.'

I really almost thought (and hoped) that that young lady would have kissed me.

'Papa always says it is a free country,' she exclaimed, 'but I never felt it to be the case before this moment.'

For years this beautiful and accomplished creature had locked this awful secret in her innocent breast—that she didn't see much fun in 'John Gilpin.' 'You have given me courage,' she said, 'to confess something else. Mr. Caldecott has just been illustrating in the same charming manner Goldsmith's "Elegy on a Mad Dog," and—I'm very sorry—but I never laughed at *that* before, either. I have pretended to laugh, you know,' she added, hastily and apologetically, 'hundreds of times.'

'I don't doubt it,' I replied; 'this is not such a free country as your father supposes.'

'But am I right?'

'I say nothing about "right,"' I answered, 'except that everybody has a right to his own opinion. For my part, however, I think the 'Mad Dog' better than 'John Gilpin' only because it is shorter.'

Whether I was wrong or right in the matter is of no consequence even to myself; the affection and gratitude of that young creature would more than repay me for a much greater mistake, if mistake it is. She protests that I have emancipated her from slavery. She has since talked to me about all sorts of authors, from Sir Philip Sidney to Washington Irving, in a way that would make some people's blood run cold; but it has no such effect upon me—quite the reverse. Of Irving she naïvely remarks that his strokes of humour seem to her to owe much of their success to the rarity of their occurrence; the flashes of fun are spread over pages of dulness, which enhance them, just as a dark night is propitious to fireworks, or the atmosphere of the House cf Commons, or of a Court of Law, to a joke. She is often in error, no doubt, but how bright and wholesome such talk is as compared with the platitudes and commonplaces which one hears on all sides in connection with literature!

As a rule, I suppose, even people in society ('the drawing-rooms and the clubs') are not absolutely base and yet one would really think so, to judge by the fear that is entertained by them of being natural. 'I vow to heaven,' says the prince of letter-writers, 'that I think the Parrots of Society are more intolerable and mischievous than its Birds of Prey. If ever I destroy myself, it will be in the bitterness of having those infernal and damnable "good old times" extolled.' One is almost tempted to say the same—when one hears their praises come from certain mouths—of the good old books. It is not everyone, of course, who has an opinion of his own upon any subject, far less on that of literature, but everyone can abstain from expressing an opinion that is not his own. If one has no voice, what possible compensation can there be in becoming an echo? No one, I conclude, would wish to see literature discoursed about in the same pinchbeck and affected style as are painting and music; [3] yet that is what will happen if this prolific weed of sham admiration is permitted to attain its full growth.

[3] The slang of art-talk has reached the 'young men' in the furniture warehouses. A friend of mine was recommended a sideboard the other day as not being a Chippendale, but as 'having a Chippendale *feeling* in it.'

THE PINCH OF POVERTY.

In these days of reduction of rents, or of total abstinence from rent-paying, it is, I am told, the correct thing to be 'a little pressed for money.' It is a sign of connection with the landed interest (like the banker's ejaculation in 'Middlemarch') and suggests family acres, and entails, and a position in the county. (In which case I know a good many people who are landlords on a very extensive scale, and have made allowances for their tenants the generosity of which may be described as Quixotic.) But as a general rule, and in times less exceptionally hard, though Shakespeare tells us 'How apt the poor are to be proud,' they are not proud of being poor.

'Poverty,' says the greatest of English divines, 'is indeed despised and makes men contemptible; it exposes a man to the influences of evil persons, and leaves a man defenceless; it is always suspected; its stories are accounted lies, and all its counsels follies; it puts a man from all employment; it makes a man's discourses tedious and his society troublesome. This is the worst of it.' Even so poverty seems pretty bad, but, begging Dr. Jeremy Taylor's pardon, what he has stated is by no means 'the worst of it.' To be in want of food at any time, and of firing in winter time, is ever so much worse than the inconveniences he enumerates; and to see those we love—delicate women and children perhaps—in want, is worse still. The fact is, the excellent bishop probably never knew what it was to go without his meals, but took them 'reg'lar' (as Mrs. Gamp took her Brighton ale) as bishops generally do. Moreover, since his day, Luxury has so universally increased, and the value of Intelligence has become so well recognised (by the publishers) that even philosophers, who profess to despise such things, have plenty to eat, and good of its kind too. Hence it happens that, from all we hear to the contrary from the greatest thinkers, the deprivation of food is a small thing: indeed, as compared with the great spiritual struggles of noble minds, and the doubts that beset them as to the supreme government of the universe, it seems hardly worth mentioning.

In old times, when folks were not so 'cultured,' starvation was thought more of. It is quite curious, indeed, to contrast the high-flying morality of the present day (when no one is permitted, either by Evolutionist or Ritualist, however dire may be his necessity, so much as to jar his conscience) with the shocking laxity of the Holy Scriptures. 'Men do not despise a thief if he steal to satisfy his soul when he is hungry,' says Solomon, after which stretch of charity, strange to say, he goes on to speak of marital infidelity in terms that, considering the number of wives he had himself, strike one as severe.

It is certain, indeed, that the sacred writers were apt to make great allowances for people with empty stomachs, and though I am well aware that the present profane ones think this very reprehensible, I venture to agree with the sacred writers. The sharpest tooth of poverty is felt, after all, in the bite of hunger. A very amusing and graphic writer once described his experience of a whole night passed in the streets; the exhaustion, the pain, the intolerable weariness of it, were set forth in a very striking manner; the sketch was called 'The Key of the Street,' and was thought by many, as Browning puts it, to be 'the true Dickens.' But what are even the pangs of sleeplessness and fatigue compared with those of want? Of course there have been fanatics who have fasted many days; but they have been supported by the prospect of spiritual reward. I confess I reserve my pity for those who have no such golden dreams, and who fast perforce. It is exceedingly difficult for mere worldlings—such as most of us are—not to eat, if it is possible, when we are hungry. I have known a great social philosopher who flattered himself that he was giving his sons an experience of High Thinking and Low Living by restricting their pocket-money to two shillings a day, out of which it was understood they were to find their own meals. I don't know whether the spirit in their case was willing, but the flesh was decidedly weak, for one of them, on this very moderate allowance, used to contrive to always have a pint of dry champagne with his luncheon. The fact is, that of the iron grip of poverty, people in general, by no means excepting those who have written about it, have had very little experience; whereas of the pinch of it a good many people know something. It is the object of this paper—and the question should be an interesting one, considering how much it is talked about—to inquire briefly where it lies.

It is quite extraordinary how very various are the opinions entertained on this point, and, before sifting them, one must be careful in the first place to eliminate from our inquiry the cases of that considerable class of persons who pinch themselves. For, however severely they do it, they may stop when they like and the pain is cured. There is all the difference in the world between pulling one's own tooth out, and even the best and kindest of dentists doing it for one. How gingerly one goes to work, and how often it strikes one that the tooth is a good tooth, that it has been a fast friend to us for ever so many years and never 'fallen out' before, and that after all it had better stop where it is!

To the truly benevolent mind, indeed, nothing is more satisfactory than to hear of a miser denying himself the necessaries of life a little too far and ridding us of his presence altogether. Our confidence in the average virtue of humanity assures us that his place will be supplied by a better man. The details of his penurious habits, the comfortless room, the scanty bedding, the cheese-rinds on his table, and the fat banking-book under his thin bolster, only inspire disgust: if he were pinched to death he did it himself, and so much the better for the world in general and his heir in particular.

Again, the people who have a thousand a year, and who try to persuade the world that they have two thousand, suffer a good deal of inconvenience, but it can't be called the pinch of poverty. They may put limits to their washing-bills, which persons of cleanlier habits would consider unpleasantly narrow; they may eat cold mutton in private for five days a week in order to eat turtle and venison in public (and with the air of eating them every day) on the sixth; and they may immure themselves in their back rooms in London throughout the autumn in order to persuade folks that they are still at Trouville, where for ten days they did really reside and in splendour; but all their stint and self-incarceration, so far from awakening pity, only fill us with contempt. I am afraid that even the complaining tones of our City friend who tells us that in consequence of 'the present unsettled state of the markets' he has been obliged to make 'great retrenchments'—which it seems on inquiry consist in putting down one of his carriages and keeping three horses instead of six—fail to draw the sympathising tear. Indeed, to a poor man this pretence of suffering on the part of the rich is perhaps even more offensive than their boasts of their prosperity.

On the other hand, when the rich become really poor their case is hard indeed; though, strange to say, we hear little of it. It is like drowning; there is a feeble cry, a little ineffectual assistance from the bystanders, and then they go under. It is not a question of pinch with *them*; they have fallen into the gaping mouth of ruin, and it has devoured them. If we ever see them again, it is in the second generation as waiters (upon Providence), or governesses, and we say, 'Why, dear me, that was Bullion's son (or daughter), wasn't it?' using the past tense, as if they were dead. 'I remember him when he lived in Eaton Square.' This class of cases rarely comes under the head of 'genteel poverty.' They were at the top, and hey presto! by some malignant stroke of fate they are at the bottom; and there they stick.

I don't believe in bachelors ever experiencing the pinch of poverty; I have heard them complaining of it at the club, while ordering Medina oysters instead of Natives, but, after all, what does it signify even if they were reduced to cockles? They have no appearances to keep up, and if they cannot earn enough to support themselves they must be poor creatures indeed.

It is the large families of moderate income, who are delicate, and have delicate tastes, that feel the twinge: and especially the poor girls. I remember a man, with little care for his personal appearance, of small means but with a very rich sense of humour, describing to me his experiences when staying at a certain ducal house in the country, where his feelings must have been very similar to those of Christopher Sly. In particular he drew a charming picture of the magnificent attendant who in the morning *would* put out his clothes for him, which had not been made by Mr. Poole, nor very recently by anybody. The contempt which he well understood his Grace's gentleman must have felt for him afforded him genuine enjoyment. But with young ladies, in a similar position, matters are very different; they have rarely a sense of humour, and certainly none strong enough to counteract the force of a personal humiliation. I have known some very charming ones, compelled to dress on a very small allowance, who, in certain mansions where they have been occasionally guests, have been afraid to put their boots outside their door, because they were not of the newest, and have trembled when the officious lady's-maid has meddled with their scanty wardrobe. A philosopher may think nothing of this, but, considering the tender skin of the sufferer, it may be fairly called a pinch.

In the investigation of this interesting subject, I have had a good deal of conversation with young ladies, who have given me the fullest information, and in a manner so charming, that, if it were common in witnesses generally, it would make Blue-Books very pretty reading.

'I consider it to be "a pinch,"' says one, 'when I am obliged to put on black mittens on occasions when I know other girls will have long white kid gloves.' I must confess I have a prejudice myself against mittens; they are, so to speak, 'gritty' to touch; so that the pinch, if it be one, experienced by the wearer, is shared by her ungloved friends. The same thing may be said of that drawing-room fire which is lit so late in the season for economical reasons, and so late in the day at all times: the pinch is felt as much by the visitors as by the members of the household. These things, however, are mere nips, and may be placed in the same category with the hardships complained of by my friend Quiverfull's second boy. 'I don't mind having papa's clothes cut up for me,' he says, 'but what I do think hard is getting Bob's clothes' (Bob being his elder brother), 'which have been papa's first; however, I am in great hopes that I am out-growing Bob.'

A much more severe example of the pinch of poverty than these is to be found in railway travelling; no lady of any sense or spirit objects to travel by the second, or even the third class, if her means do not justify her going by the first. But when she meets with richer friends upon the platform, and parts with them to journey in the same compartment with their man-servant, she suffers as acutely as though, when the guard slams the door of the carriage with the vehemence proportioned to its humble rank, her tender hand had been crushed in it. Of course it is very foolish of her; but it demands democratic opinions, such as almost no woman of birth and breeding possesses, not to feel *that* pinch. Her knowledge that it is also hard upon the man-servant, who has never sat in her presence before, but only stooped over her shoulder with "Ock, miss,' serves but to increase her pain.

A great philosopher has stated that the worst evil of poverty is, that it makes folks ridiculous; by which, I hope, he only means that, as in the above case, it places them in incongruous positions. The man, or woman, who derives amusement from the lack of means of a fellow-creature, would jeer at a natural deformity, be cruel to children, and insult old age. Such people should be whipped and then hanged. Nevertheless there are certain little pinches of poverty so slight, that they tickle almost as much as they hurt the victim. A lady once told me (interrupting herself, however, with pleasant bursts of merriment) that as a young girl her allowance was so small that when she went out to spend the evening at a friend's, her promised pleasure was darkened by the presentiment (always fulfilled) that the cabman was sure to charge her more than the proper fare. The extra expense was really of consequence to her, but she never dared dispute it, because of the presence of the footman who opened the door.

Some young ladies—quite as lady-like as any who roll in chariots—cannot even afford a cab. 'What *I* call the pinch of poverty,' observed an example of this class, 'is the waiting for omnibus after omnibus on a wet afternoon and finding them all full.'

'But surely,' I replied with gallantry, 'any man would have given up his seat to you?'

She shook her head with a smile that had very little fun in it. 'People in omnibuses,' she said, 'don't give up their seats to others.' Nor, I am bound to confess, do they do so elsewhere; if I had been in their place, perhaps I should have been equally selfish; though I do think I should have made an effort, in this instance at least, to make room for her close beside me. [4]

[4] There is, however, some danger in this. I remember reading of some highly respectable old gentleman in the City who thus accommodated on a wet day a very nice young woman in humble circumstances. She was as full of apologies as of rainwater, and he of good-natured rejoinders, intended to put her at her ease; so that he became, in a Platonic and paternal way, quite friendly with her by the time she arrived at her destination—which happened to be his own door. She turned out to be his new cook, which was afterwards very embarrassing.

A young governess whom some wicked fairy endowed at her birth with the sensitiveness often denied to princesses, has assured me that her journeys by railway have sometimes been rendered miserable by the thought that she had not even a few pence to spare for the porter who would presently shoulder her little box on to the roof of her cab.

It is people of this class, much more than those beneath them, who are shut out from all amusements. The mechanic goes to the play and to the music-hall, and occasionally takes his 'old girl,' as he calls his wife, and even 'a kid' or two, to the Crystal Palace. But those I have in my mind have no such relaxation from compulsory duty and importunate care. 'I know it's very foolish, but I feel it sometimes to be a pinch,' says one of these ill-fated ones, 'to see them all [the daughters of her employer] going to the play, or the opera, while I am expected to be satisfied with a private view of their pretty dresses.' No doubt it is the sense of comparison (especially with the female) that sharpens the sting of poverty. It is not, however, through envy that the 'prosperity of fools destroys us,' so much as the knowledge of its unnecessariness and waste. When a mother has a sick child who needs sea air, which she cannot afford to give it, the consciousness that her neighbour's family (the head of which perhaps is a most successful financier and market-rigger) are going to the Isle of Wight for three months, though there is nothing at all the matter with them, is an added bitterness. How often it is said (no doubt with some well-intentioned idea of consolation) that after all money cannot buy life! I remember a curious instance to the contrary of this. In the old days of sailing-packets a country gentleman embarked for Ireland, and when a few miles from land broke a bloodvessel through seasickness. A doctor on board pronounced that he would certainly die before the completion of the voyage if it was continued; whereupon the sick man's friends consulted with the captain, who convoked the passengers, and persuaded them to accept compensation in proportion to their needs for allowing the vessel to be put back; which was accordingly done.

One of the most popular fictions of our time was even written with this very moral, that life is unpurchasable. Yet nothing is more certain than that life is often lost through want of money—that is, of the obvious means to save it. In such a case how truly has it been written that 'the destruction of the poor is their poverty'! This, however, is scarcely a pinch, but, to those who have hearts to feel it, a wrench that 'divides asunder the joints and the marrow.'

A nobler example, because a less personal one, of the pinch of poverty, is when it prevents the accomplishment of some cherished scheme for the benefit of the human race. I have felt such a one myself when in extreme youth I was unable, from a miserable absence of means, to publish a certain poem in several cantos. That the world may not have been much better for it if I had had the means does not affect the question. It is easy to be incredulous. Henry VII. of England did not believe in the expectations of Columbus, and suffered for it, and his case may have been similar to that of the seven publishers to whom I applied in vain.

A man with an invention on which he has spent his life, but has no means to get it developed for the good of humanity—or even patented for himself—must feel the pinch of poverty very acutely.

To sum up the matter, the longer I live, the more I am convinced that the general view in respect to material means is a false one. That great riches are a misfortune is quite true; the effect of them in the moral sense (with here and there a glorious exception, however) is deplorable: a shower of gold falling continuously upon any body (or soul) is as the waters of a petrifying spring. But, on the other hand, the occasional and precarious dripping of coppers has by no means a genial effect. If the one recipient becomes hard as the nether millstone, the other (just as after constant 'pinching' a limb becomes insensible) grows callous, and also (though it seems like a contradiction in terms) sometimes acquires a certain dreadful suppleness. Nothing is more monstrous than the generally received opinion with respect to a moderate competence; that 'fatal gift,' as it is called, which encourages idleness in youth by doing away with the necessity for exertion. I never hear the same people inveighing against great inheritances, which are much more open to such objections. The fact is, if a young man is naturally indolent, the spur of necessity will drive him but a very little way, while the having enough to live upon is often the means of preserving his self-respect. One constantly hears what humiliating things men will do for money, whereas the truth is that they do them for the want of it. It is not the temptation which induces them, but the pinch. 'Give me neither poverty nor riches,' was Agur's prayer; 'feed me with food convenient for me, lest I be full and deny Thee, and say, Who is the Lord? or lest I be poor and steal.' And there are many things—flatteries, disgraceful humiliations, hypocrisies—which are almost as bad as stealing. One of the sharpest pinches of poverty to some minds must be their inability (because of their dependency on him and that of others upon them) to tell a man what they think of him.

Riches and poverty are of course but relative terms; but the happiest material position in which a man can be placed is that of 'means with a margin.' Then, however small his income may be, however it may behove him to 'cut and contrive,' as the housekeepers call it, he does not feel the pinch of poverty. I have known a rich man say to an acquaintance of this class, 'My good friend, if you only knew how very small are the pleasures my money gives me which you yourself cannot purchase!' And for once it was not one of those cheap and empty consolations which the wealthy are so ready to bestow upon their less fortunate fellow-creatures. Dives was, in that instance, quite right in his remark; only we must remember he was not speaking to Lazarus. 'A dinner of herbs where love is,' is doubtless quite sufficient for us; only there must be enough of it, and the herbs should be nicely cooked in an omelette.

THE LITERARY CALLING AND ITS FUTURE.

One would think that in writing about literary men and matters there would be no difficulty in finding a title for one's essay, or that any embarrassment which might arise would be from excess of material. I find this, however, far from being the case. 'Men of Letters,' for example, is a heading too classical and pretentious. I do indeed remember its being used in these modern days by the sub-editor of a country paper, who, having quarrelled with his proprietor, and reduced him to silence by a violent kick in the abdomen, thus addressed him: 'I leave you and your dirty work for ever, and start to-night for London, to take up my proper position as a Man of Letters.' But this gentleman's case (and I hope that of his proprietor) was an exceptional one. The term in general is too ambitious and suggestive of the author of 'Cato,' for my humble purpose. 'Literature as a Profession,' again, is open to objection on the question of fact. The professions do not admit literature into their brotherhood. 'Literature, Science, and Art' are all spoken of in the lump, and rather contemptuously (like 'reading, writing, and arithmetic'), and have no settled position whatever. In a book of precedence, however—a charming class of work, and much more full of humour than the peerage—I recently found indicated for the first time the relative place of Literature in the social scale. After a long list of Eminent Personages and Notables, the mere perusal of which was calculated to bring the flush of pride into my British cheek, I found at the very bottom these remarkable words, 'Burgesses, Literary Persons, and others.' Lest haughtiness should still have any place in the breasts of these penultimates of the human race, the order was repeated in the same delightful volume in still plainer fashion, 'Burgesses, Literary Persons, etc.' It is something, of course, to take precedence—in going down to dinner, for example—even of an et cetera; but who are Burgesses? I have a dreadful suspicion they are not gentlemen. Are they ladies? Did I ever meet a Burgess, I wonder, coming through the rye? At all events, after so authoritative a statement of its social position, I feel that to speak of Literature as a profession would be an hyperbole.

On the other hand, 'The Literary Calling' is not a title that satisfies me. For the word 'calling' implies a certain fitness; in the religious sense it has even more significance; and it cannot be denied that there are a good many persons who devote—well, at least, their time to literature, who can hardly be said to have 'a call' in that direction, nor even so much as a whisper. At the same time I will venture to observe, notwithstanding a great deal of high-sounding twaddle talked and written to the contrary, that it is not necessary for a man to feel any miraculous or even extraordinary attraction to this pursuit to succeed in it very tolerably. I remember a now distinguished personage (in another line) who had written a very successful work, expressing his opinion to me that unless a certain divine afflatus animated a man, he should never take up his pen to address the public. The writing for pay, he added (he had at least £5,000 a year of his own), was the degradation of literature. As I had written about a dozen books myself at the time, and most decidedly with an eye to profit, and had never experienced much afflatus, this remark discouraged me very much. However, as the gentleman in question did essay another volume, which was so absolute and distinct a failure that he promptly took up another line of business (far above that of Burgesses), it is probable he altered his views.

Nature of course is the best guide in the matter of choosing a pursuit. When she says 'This is your line, stick to it,' she seldom or never makes a mistake. But, on the other hand, her speech must be addressed to mature ears. For my part, I do not much believe in the predilections of boyhood. I was never so simple as to wish to go to sea, but I do remember (when between seven and eight) having a passionate longing to become a merchant. I had no notion, however, of the preliminary stages; the high stool in the close street; luncheon at a counter, standing (I liked to have my meals good, plentiful, often, and in comfort, even then); and imprisonment at the office on the eves of mail nights till the large hours p.m. Even the full fruition of such aspirations—the large waistcoat beginning to 'point,' (as it soon does in merchants), heavy watchchain, and cheerful conviction of the coming scarcity of necessaries for everybody else, would have failed to please. The sort of merchant I wanted to be was never found in 'Post Office Directory,' but in the 'Arabian Nights,' trading to Bussorah, chiefly in pearls and diamonds. When the Paterfamiliases of my acquaintance instance certain stenches and messes which their Toms and Harrys make with chemicals all over their house, as a proof of 'their natural turn for engineering,' I say, 'Very likely,' or 'A capital thing,' but I *think* of that early attraction of my own towards Bussorah. The young gentlemen never dream of what I once heard described, in brief, as the real business life of a scientific apprentice: 'To lie on your back with a candle in your hand, while another fellow knocks nails into a boiler.'

Boys have rarely any special aptitude for anything practical beyond punching each others' heads, or (and these are the clever ones) for keeping their own heads unpunched. As a rule, in short, Nature is not demonstrative as respects our professional future.

It must nevertheless be conceded that if the boy is ever father to the man in this respect, it is in connection with literature. Also, however prosaic their works are fated to be, it is curious that the aspirants for the profession below Burgesses always begin with Poetry. Even Harriet Martineau wrote verses in early life bad enough to comfort the soul of any respectable parent. The approach to the Temple of Literary Fame is almost always through double gates—couplets. And yet I have known youthful poets, apparently bound for Paternoster Row, bolt off the course in a year or two, to the delight of their friends, and become, of their own free will, drysalters.

There is so much talk about the 'indications of immortality in early childhood' (of a very different kind from those referred to by Wordsworth), and it is so much the habit of biographers to use magnifiers when their subject is small, that it needs some courage to avow my belief that the tastes of boys have very little significance. A clever boy can be trained to almost anything, and an ordinary boy will not do one thing much better than another. With the Geniuses I will allow (for the sake of peace and quietness) that Nature is all-powerful, but with nine hundred and ninety-nine out of a thousand of us, Second Nature, Use, is the true mistress; and what will doubtless strike some people as almost paradoxical, but is nevertheless a fact, Literature is the calling in which she has the greatest sway.

It is the fashion with that enormous class of people who don't know what they are talking about, and who take up cuckoo-cries, to speak contemptuously of modern literature, by which they mean (for they are acquainted with little else) periodical literature. However small may be its merits, it is at all events ten times as good as ancient periodical literature used to be. A very much better authority than myself on such a subject has lately informed us that the majority of the old essays in the *Edinburgh Review*, at the very time when it was supposed to be most 'trenchant,' 'masterly,' 'exhaustive,' and a number of other splendid epithets, are so dull and weak and ignorant, that it is impossible that they or their congeners would now find acceptance in any periodical of repute. And with regard to all other classes of old magazine literature, this verdict is certainly most just.

Let us take what most people suppose to be 'the extreme case,' Magazine Poetry. Of course there is to-day a great deal of rant and twaddle published under the name of verse in magazines; yet I could point to scores and scores of poems that have thus appeared during the last ten years,[5] which half a century ago would have made—and deservedly have made—a high reputation for their authors. Such phrases as 'universal necessity for practical exertion,' 'prosaic character of the age,' etc., are, of course, common enough; but those who are acquainted with such matters will, I am sure, corroborate my assertion that there was never so much good poetry in our general literature as exists at present. Persons of intelligence do not look for such things perhaps, and certainly not in magazines, while persons of 'culture' are too much occupied with old china and high art; but to humble folks, who take an interest in their fellow-creatures, it is very pleasant to observe what high thoughts, and how poetically expressed, are now to be found about our feet, and, as it were, in the literary gutter. I don't compare these writers with Byrons and Shelleys; I don't speak of them as born poets at all. On the contrary, my argument is that second nature (cultivation, opportunities of publication, etc.) has made them what they are; and it is immensely creditable to her.

And what holds good of verse holds infinitely better in respect to prose. The enormous improvement in our prose writers (I am not speaking of geniuses, remember, but of the generality), and their great superiority over writers of the same class half a century ago, is mainly due to use. Sir Walter Scott, who, like most men of genuine power, had great generosity, once observed to a brother author, 'You and I came just in the nick of time.' He foresaw the formidable competition that was about to take place, though he had no cause to fear it. I think in these days he would have had cause; not that I disbelieve in his genius, but that I venture to think he diffused it over too large an area. In such cases genius is overpassed by the talent which husbands its resources; in other words, Nature succumbs to second nature, as the wife in the patriarchal days (when *she* grew patriarchal) succumbed to the handmaid. And after all, though we talk so glibly about genius, and profess to feel, though we cannot express, in what it differs from talent, are we quite so sure about this as we would fain persuade ourselves? At all events, it cannot surely be contended that a man of genius always writes like one; and when he does not, his work is often inferior to the first-rate production of a man of talent. For my own part, I am not sure whether (with the exception, perhaps, of the highest gifts of song) the whole distinction is not fanciful.

We are ready enough in ordinary matters to allow that 'practice makes perfect,' and the limit of that principle is yet to be found. Moreover, the vast importance of exclusive application is almost unknown. We see it, indeed, in men of science and in lawyers, but without recognition; nay, socially, it is even quoted against them. The mathematician may be very eminent, but we find him dry; the lawyer may be at the head of his profession, but we find him dull; and it is observed on all sides how very little great A and great B, notwithstanding the high position they have earned for themselves in their calling, know of matters out of their own line. On the other hand, the man of whom it was said that 'science was his forte and omniscience his foible,' has left no enduring monument behind him; and so it must always be with mortals who have only fifty years of thought allotted to them at the very most, and who diffuse it. Everyone admits the value of application, but very few are aware how its force is wasted by diffusion: it is like a volatile essence in a bottle without a cork. When, on the other hand, it is concentrated—you may call it 'narrowed' if you please—there is hardly anything within its own sphere of action of which it is not capable. So many high motives (though also some mean ones) prompt us to make broad the bases of education, that any proposal to contract them must needs be thankless and unpopular; but it is certain that, among the upper classes at least, the reason why so many men are unable to make their way in the world, is because, thanks to a too liberal education, they are Jacks of all trades and masters of none; and even as Jacks they cut a very poor figure.

How large and varied is the educational bill of fare set before every young gentleman in Great Britain; and to judge by the mental stamina it affords him in most cases, what a waste of good food it is! The dishes are so numerous and so quickly changed, that he has no time to decide on which he likes best. Like an industrious flea, rather than a bee, he hops from flower to flower in the educational garden, without one penny-worth of honey to show for it. And then—though I feel how degrading it is to allude to so vulgar a matter—how high is the price of admission to the feast in question! Its purveyors do not pretend to have filled his stomach, but only to have put him in the way of filling it for himself, whereas, unhappily, Paterfamilias discovers that that is the very thing that they have not done. His young Hopeful at twenty-one is almost as unable to run alone as when he first entered the nursery. To discourse airily upon the beauties of classical education, and on the social advantages of acquiring 'the tone' at a public school at whatever cost, is an agreeable exercise of the intelligence; but such arguments have been taken too seriously, and the result is that our young gentlemen are incapable of gaining their own living. It is not only that 'all the gates are thronged with suitors, all the markets overflow,' but even when the candidates are so fortunate as to attain admittance, they are still a burden upon their fathers for years, from having had no especial preparation for the work they have to do. Folks who can afford to spend £250 a year on their sons at Eton or Harrow, and to add another fifty or two for their support at the universities, do not feel this; but those who have done it without affording it—*i.e.*, by cutting and contriving, if not by pinching and saving—feel their position very bitterly. There are hundreds of clever young men who are now living at home and doing nothing—or work that pays nothing, and even costs something for doing it—who might be earning very tolerable incomes by their pen if they only knew how, and had not wasted their young wits on Greek plays and Latin verses; nor do I find that the attractions of such objects of study are permanent, or afford the least solace to these young gentlemen in their enforced leisure.

The idea of bringing young people up to Literature is doubtless calculated to raise the eyebrows almost as much as the suggestion of bringing them up to the Stage. The notions of Paterfamilias in this respect are very much what they were fifty years ago. 'What! put my boy in Grub Street? I would rather see him in his coffin.' In his mind's eye he beholds Savage on his bunk and Chatterton on his deathbed. He does not know that there are many hundreds of persons of both sexes who have found out this vocation for themselves, and are diligently pursuing it—under circumstances of quite unnecessary difficulty—to their material advantage. He is unaware that the conditions of literature in England have been as completely changed within a single generation as those of locomotion.

There are, it is true, at present no great prizes in literature such as are offered by the learned professions, but there are quite as many small ones—competences; while, on the other hand, it is not so much of a lottery. It is not necessary to marry an attorney's daughter, or a bishop's, to get on in it. The calling, as it is termed (I know not why, for it is often heavy enough), of 'light literature' is in such contempt, through ignorance on the one hand, and arrogance on the other, that one is almost afraid in such a connection to speak of merit; yet merit, or, at all events, aptitude with diligence, is certain of success in it. A great deal has been said about editors being blind to the worth of unknown authors; but if so, they must be also blind (and this I have never heard said of them) to their own interests. It would be just as reasonable to accuse a recruiting sergeant of passing by the stout six-feet fellows who wish to enlist with him, and for each of whom—directly or indirectly—he receives head-money. It is possible, of course, that one particular sergeant may be drunken, or careless of his own interests, but in that case the literary recruit has only to apply next door. The opportunities for action in the field of literature are now so very numerous that it is impossible that any able volunteer should be long shut out of it; and I have observed that the complaints about want of employment come almost solely from those unfit for service. Nay, in the ranks of the literaryarmy there are very many who should have been excluded. Few, if any, are there through favour; but the fact is, the work to be done is so extensive and so varied, that there is not a sufficiency of good candidates to do it. And of what is called 'skilled labour' among them there is scarcely any.

The question 'What can you do?' put by an editor to an aspirant, generally astonishes him very much. The aspirant is ready to do anything, he says, which the other will please to suggest. 'But what is your line in literature? What can you do best—not tragedies in blank verse, I hope?' Perhaps the aspirant here hangs his head; he *has* written tragedies. In which case there is good hope for him, because it shows a natural bent. But he generally replies that he has written nothing as yet except that essay on the genius of Cicero (at which the editor has already shaken his head), and that defence of Mary Queen of Scots. Or perhaps he has written some translations of Horace, which he is surprised to find not a novelty; or some considerations upon the value of a feudal system. At four-and-twenty, in short, he is but an overgrown schoolboy. He has been taught, indeed, to acquire knowledge of a certain sort, but not the habit of acquiring; he has been taught to observe nothing; he is ignorant upon all the subjects that interest his fellow-creatures, and in his new ambition is like one who endeavours to attract an audience without having anything to tell them. He knows some Latin, a little Greek, a very little French, and a very very little of what are called the English classics. He has read a few recent novels perhaps, but of modern English literature, and of that (to him at least) most important branch of it, English journalism, he knows nothing. His views and opinions are those of a public school, which are by no means in accordance with those of the great world of readers; or he is full of the class prejudices imbibed at college. In short, he may be as vigorous as a Zulu, with the materials of a first-rate soldier in him, but his arms are only a club and an assegai, and are of no service. Why should he not be fitted out in early life with literary weapons of precision, and taught the use of them?

I say, again, that poor Paterfamilias looking hopelessly about him, like Quintus Curtius in the riddle, for 'a nice opening for a young man,' is totally ignorant of the opportunities, if not for fame and fortune, at least for competency and comfort, that Literature now offers to a clever lad. He looks round him; he sees the Church leading nowhere, with much greater certainty of expense than income, and demanding a huge sum for what is irreverently termed 'gate money;' he sees the Bar, with its high road leading indeed to the woolsack, but with a hundred by-ways leading nowhere in particular, and full of turnpikes—legal tutors, legal fees, rents of chambers, etc.—which he has to defray; he sees Physic, at which Materfamilias sniffs and turns her nose up. 'Her Jack, with such agreeable manners, to become a saw-bones! Never!' He sees the army, and thinks, since Jack has such great abilities, it seems a pity to give him a red coat, which costs also considerably more than a black one; And how is Jack to live upon his pay?

After all, indeed, however prettily one puts it, the question is with him, not so much '*What* is my Jack to be?' as '*How* is my Jack to live?' To one who has any gift of humour there are few things more amusing than to observe how this vulgar, but really rather important inquiry, is ignored by those who take the subject of modern education in hand. They are chiefly schoolmasters, who are not so deep in their books but that they can spare a glance or two in the direction of their banker's account; or fellows of colleges who have no children, and therefore never feel the difficulties of supporting them. Heaven forbid that so humble an individual as myself should question their wisdom, or say anything about them that should seem to smack of irreverence; but I do believe that (with one or two exceptions I have in my mind) the system they have introduced among us is the Greatest Humbug in the universe. In the meantime poor Paterfamilias (who is the last man, they flatter themselves, to find this out) stands with his hands (and very little else) in his pockets, regarding his clever offspring, and wondering what he shall do with him. He remembers to have read about a man on his deathbed, who calls his children about him and thanks God, though he has left them nothing to live upon, he has given them a good education, and tries to extract comfort from the reminiscence. That he has spent money enough upon Jack's education is certain; something between two or three thousand pounds in all at least, the interest of which, it strikes him, would be very convenient just now to keep him. But unfortunately the principal is gone and Jack isn't.

Now suppose—for one may suppose anything, however ridiculous—he had spent two or three hundred pounds at the very most, and brought him up to the Calling of Literature. He believes, perhaps, that it is only geniuses that succeed in it (in which case I know more geniuses than I had any idea of), and he doesn't think Jack a genius, though Jack's mother does. Or, as is more probable, he regards it as a hand-to-mouth calling, which to-day gives its disciples a five-pound note, and to-morrow five pence. He calls to mind a saying about Literature being a good stick, but not a good crutch—an excellent auxiliary, but no permanent support; but he forgets the all-important fact that the remark was made half a century ago.

Poor blind Paterfamilias—shall I couch you? If the operation is successful, I am sure you will thank me for it; but, on the other hand, I foresee I shall incur the greatest enmities. Should I encourage clever Jack, and, what is worse, a thousand Jacks who are not clever, to enter upon this vocation, what will editors say to me? I shall have to go about, perhaps, guarded with two policemen with revolvers, like an Irish gentleman on his landed estate. 'Is not the flood of rubbish to which we are already subjected,' I hear them crying, 'bad enough, without your pulling up the sluices of universal stupidity?' My suggestion, however, is intended to benefit them by clearing away the rubbish, and inducing a clearer and deeper stream for the turning of their mills. At the same time I confess that the lessening of Paterfamilias's difficulties is my main object. What I would open his eyes to is the fact that a calling, of the advantages of which he has no knowledge, *does* present itself to clever Jack, which will cost him nothing but pens, ink, and paper to enter upon, and in which, if he has been well trained for it, he will surely be successful, since so many succeed in it without any training at all. Why should not clever Jack have this in view as much as the *ignes fatui* of woolsacks and mitres? If it has no lord chancellorships, it has plenty of county court appointments; if it has no bishoprics, it has plenty of benefices—and really, as times go, some pretty fat ones.

On your breakfast-table, good Paterfamilias, there lies, every morning, a newspaper, and on Saturday perhaps there are two or three. When you go out in the street, you are pestered to buy half a score more of them. In your club reading-room there are a hundred different journals. When you travel by the railway you see at every station a provincial newspaper of more or less extensive circulation. Has it never struck you that to supply these publications with their leading articles, there must be an immense staff of persons called journalists, professing every description of opinion, and advocating every conceivable policy? And do you suppose these gentry only get £70 a year for their work, like a curate; or £60, like a sub-lieutenant; or that they have to pay three times those sums for the privilege of belonging to the press, as a barrister does for belonging to his inn? Again, in London at least, there are as many magazines as newspapers, containing every kind of literature, the very contributors of which are so numerous, that they form a public of themselves. That seems at the first blush to militate against my suggestion, but though contributors are so common, and upon the whole so good—indeed, considering the conditions under which they labour, so wonderfully good—they are not (I have heard editors say) so good as they might be, supposing (for example) they knew a little of science, history, politics, English literature, and especially of the art of composition, before they volunteered their services. At present the ranks of journalistic and periodical literature are largely recruited from the failures in other professions. The bright young barrister who can't get a brief takes to literature as a calling, just as the man who has 'gone a cropper' in the army takes to the wine-trade. And what æons of time, and what millions of money, have been wasted in the meanwhile!

The announcement written on the gates of all the recognised professions in England is the same that would-be travellers read on the faces of the passengers on the underground railway after office hours: 'Our number is complete, and our room is limited.' In literature, on the contrary, though its vehicles may seem as tightly packed, substitution can be effected. There may be persons travelling on that line in the first-class who ought to be in the third, and indeed have no reasonable pretext for being there at all. And if clever Jack could show his ticket, he would turn them out of it.

Again, so far from the space being limited, it is continually enlarging, and that out of all proportion to those who have tickets. We hear from its enemies that the Church is doomed, and from its friends that it is in danger; there is a small but energetic party who are bent on reducing the Army, and even on doing away with it; nay, so wicked and presumptuous has human nature grown, that mutterings are heard and menaces uttered against the delay and exactions of the Law itself; whereas Literature has no foes, and is enlarging its boundaries in all directions. It is all 'a-growing and a-blowing,' as the peripatetic gardeners say of their plants; but, unlike their wares, it has its roots deep in the soil and is an evergreen. Its promise is golden, and its prospects are boundless for every class of writer.

In some excellent articles on Modern Literature in *Blackwood's Magazine* the other day, this subject was touched upon with respect to fiction, and might well have filled a greater space, for the growth of that description of literature of late years is simply marvellous. Curiously enough, though France originated the *feuilleton*, it was from America and our own colonies that England seems to have taken the idea of publishing novels in newspapers. It was a common practice in Australia long before we adopted it; and, what is also curious, it was first acclimatised among us by our provincial papers. The custom is rapidly gaining ground in London, but in the country there is now scarcely any newspaper of repute which does not enlist the aid of fiction to attract its readers. Many of them are contented with very poor stuff, for which they pay a proportional price; but others club together with other newspapers—the operation has even received the technical term of 'forming a syndicate'—and are thereby enabled to secure the services of popular authors; while the newspapers thus arranged for are published at a good distance from one another, so as not to interfere with each other's circulation. Country journals, which are not so ambitious, instead of using an inferior article, will often purchase the 'serial right,' as it is called, of stories which have already appeared elsewhere, or have passed through the circulating libraries. Nay, the novelist who has established a reputation has many more strings to his bow: his novel, thus published in the country newspapers, also appears coincidently in the same serial shape in Australia, Canada, and other British colonies, leaving the three-volume form and the cheap editions 'to the good.' And what is true of fiction is in a less degree true of other kinds of literature. Travels are 'gutted,' and form articles in magazines, illustrated by the original plates; lectures, after having served their primary purpose, are published in a similar manner; even scientific works now appear first in the magazines which are devoted to science before performing their mission of 'popularising' their subject.

When speaking of the growth of readers, I have purposely not mentioned America. For the present the absence of copyright there is destroying both author and publisher; but the wheels of justice, though tardy, are making way there. In a few years that great continent of readers will be legitimately added to the audience of the English author, and those that have stolen will steal no more.

Nor, in our own country, must we fail to take notice of the establishment of School Boards. A generation hence we shall have a reading public almost as numerous as in America; even the very lowest classes will have acquired a certain culture which will beget demands both for journalists and 'literary persons.' The harvest will be plenteous indeed, but unless my advice be followed in some shape or another, the labourers will be comparatively few and superlatively inadequate.

I am well aware how mischievous, as well as troublesome, would be the encouragement of mediocrity; and in stating these promising facts I have no such purpose in my mind. On the contrary, there is an immense amount of mediocrity already in literature, which I think my proposition of training up 'clever Jack' to that calling would discourage. I have no expectation of establishing a manufactory for genius—and indeed, for reasons it is not necessary to specify, I would not do it if I could. But whereas all kinds of 'culture' have been recommended to the youth of Great Britain (and certainly with no limit as to the expense of acquisition), the cultivation of such natural faculties as imagination and humour (for example) has never been suggested. The possibility of such a thing will doubtless be denied. I am quite certain, however, that they are capable of great development, and that they may be brought to attain, if not perfection, at all events a high degree of excellence. The proof, to those who choose to look for it, is plain enough even as matters stand. Use and opportunity are already producing scores of examples of it; if supplemented by early education they might surely produce still more.

There is so great and general a prejudice against special studies, that I must humbly conclude there is something in it. On the other hand, I know a large number of highly—that is broadly—educated persons, who are desperately dull. 'But would they have been less dull,' it may be asked, 'if they were also ignorant?' Yes, I believe they would. They have swallowed too much for digestions naturally weak; they have become inert, conceited, oppressive to themselves and others—Prigs. And I think that even clever young people suffer in a less degree from the same cause. Some one has written, 'Information is always useful.' This reminds me of the married lady, fond of bargains, who once bought a door-plate at a sale with 'Mr. Wilkins' on it. Her own name was Jones, but the doorplate was very cheap, and her husband, she argued, *might* die, and then she might marry a man of the name of Wilkins. 'Depend upon it, everything comes in useful,' she said, 'if you only keep it long enough.'

This is what I venture to doubt. I have myself purchased several door-plates (quite as burthensome, but not so cheap as that good lady's), which have been of no sort of use to me, and are still on hand.

[5] I take up a half-yearly volume of a magazine (price 1½d. weekly) addressed to the middle classes, and find in it, at haphazard, the five following pieces, the authors of which are anonymous:

AGATHA.

'From under the shade of her simple straw hat
She smiles at you, only a little shamefaced:
Her gold-tinted hair m a long-braided plait
Reaches on either side down to her waist.
Her rosy complexion, a soft pink and white,
Except where the white has been warmed by the sun,
Is glowing with health and an eager delight,
As she pauses to speak to you after her run.

'See with what freedom, what beautiful ease,
She leaps over hollows and mounds in berrace;
Hear how she joyously laughs when the breeze
Tosses her hat off, and blows in her face!
It's only a play-gown of homeliest cotton
She wears, that her finer silk dress may be saved;
And happily, too, she has wholly forgotten
The nurse and her charge to be better behaved.

'Must a time come when this child's way of caring
For only the present enjoyment shall pass;
When she'll learn to take thought of the dress that she's wearing,
And grow rather fond of consulting the glass?
Well, never mind; nothing really can change her;
Fair childhood will grow to as fair maidenhood;
Her unselfish, sweet nature is safe from all danger;
I know she will always be charming and good.

'For when she takes care of a still younger brother,
You see her stop short in the midst of her mirth,
Gravely and tenderly playing the mother:
Can there be anything fairer on earth?
So proud of her charge she appears, so delighted;
Of all her perfections (indeed, they're a host),
This loving attention to others, united
With naive self-unconsciousness, charms me the most.

'What hearts that unthinkingly under short jackets
Are beating to-day in a wonderful wise
About racing, or jumping, or cricket, or rackets,
One day will beat at a smile from those eyes!
Ah, how I envy the one that shall win her,
And see that sweet smile no ill-humour shall damp,
Shining across the spread table at dinner,
Or cheerfully bright in the light of the lamp.

'Ah, little fairy! a very short while,
Just once or twice, in a brief country stay,
I saw you; but when will your innocent smile
That I keep in my mem'ry have faded away?
For when, in the midst of my trouble and doubt,
I remember your face with its laughter and light,
It's as if on a sudden the sun had shone out,
And scattered the shadow, and made the world bright.'

CHARTREUSE.

(*Liqueur.*)

'Who could refuse
Green-eyed Chartieuse?

Liquor for heretics,
Turks, Christians, or Jews
For beggar or queen,
For monk or for dean;

Ripened and mellow
(The *green*, not the yellow),
Give it its dues,
Gay little fellow,
Dressed up in green!
I love thee too well, O
Laughing Chartreuse!

'O the delicate hues
That thrill through the green!
Colours which Greuze
Would die to have seen!
With thee would De Musset
Sweeten his muse;
Use, not abuse,
Bright little fellow!
(The green, *not* the yellow.)
O the taste and the smell! O
Never refuse
A kiss on the lips from
Jealous Chartreuse!'

THE LIFE-LEDGER.

'Our sufferings we reckon o'er
With skill minute and formal;
The cheerful ease that fills the score

We treat as merely normal.
Our list of ills, how full, how great!
We mourn our lot should fall so;
I wonder, do we calculate
Our happinesses also?

'Were it not best to keep account
Of all days, if of any?
Perhaps the dark ones might amount
To not so very many.
Men's looks are nigh as often gay
As sad, or even solemn:
Behold, my entry for to-day
Is in the "happy" column.'

OCTOBER.

'The year grows old; summer's wild crown of roses
Has fallen and faded in the woodland ways;
On all the earth a tranquil light reposes,
Through the still dreamy days.

'The dew lies heavy in the early morn,
On grass and mosses sparkling crystal-fair;
And shining threads of gossamer are borne
Floating upon the air,

'Across the leaf-strewn lanes, from bough to bough
Like tissue woven in a fairy loom;
And crimson-berried bryony garlands glow
Through the leaf-tangled gloom.

'The woods are still, but for the sudden fall

Of cupless acorns dropping to the ground,
Or rabbit plunging through the fern-stems tall,
Half-startled by the sound.

'And from the garden lawn comes, soft and clear,
The robin's warble from the leafless spray,
The low sweet Angelus of the dying year,
Passing in light away.'

PROSPERITY.

'I doubt if the maxims the Stoic adduces
Be true in the main, when they state
That our nature's improved by adversity's uses,
And spoilt by a happier fate.

'The heart that is tried by misfortune and pain,
Self-reliance and patience may learn;
Yet worn by long waiting and wishing in vain,
It often grows callous and stern.

'But the heart that is softened by ease and contentment,
Feels warmly and kindly t'wards all;
And its charity, roused by no moody resentment,
Embraces alike great and small.

'So, although in the season of rain-storms and showers,
The tree may strike deeper its roots,
It needs the warm brightness of sunshiny hours
To ripen the blossoms and fruits.'

Observe, not only the genuine merit of these five pieces, but the variety in the tones of thought: then compare them with similar productions of the days, say, of the once famous L.E.L.

STORY-TELLING.

The most popular of English authors has given us an account of what within his experience (and it was a large one) was the impression among the public at large of the manner in which his work was done. They pictured him, he says,

as a radiant personage whose whole time is devoted to idleness and pastime; who keeps a prolific mind in a sort of corn-sieve and lightly shakes a bushel of it out sometimes in an odd half-hour after breakfast. It would amaze their incredulity beyond all measure to" be told that such elements as patience, study, punctuality, determination, self-denial, training of mind and body, hours of application and seclusion to produce what they read in seconds, enter in such a career ... correction and recorrection in the blotted manuscript; consideration; new observations; the patient massing of many reflections, experiences, and imaginings for one minute purpose; and the patient separation from the heap of all the fragments that will unite to serve it—these would be unicorns and griffins to them—fables altogether.

And as it was, a quarter of a century ago, when those words were written, so it is now: the phrase of 'light literature' as applied to fiction having once been invented, has stuck, with a vengeance, to those who profess it.

Yet to 'make the thing that is not as the thing that is' is not (though it may seem to be the same thing) so easy as lying.

Among a host of letters received in connection with an article published in the *Nineteenth Century*, entitled 'The Literary Calling and its Future,' and which testify in a remarkable manner to the pressing need (therein alluded to) of some remunerative vocation among the so-called educated classes, there are many which are obviously written under the impression that Dogberry's view of writing coming 'by nature' is especially true of the writing of fiction. Because I ventured to hint that the study of Greek was not essential to the calling of a story-teller, or of a contributor to the periodicals, or even of a journalist, these gentlemen seem to jump to the conclusion that the less they know of anything the better. Nay, some of them, discarding all theories (in the fashion that Mr. Carlyle's heroes are wont to discard all formulas), proceed to the practical with quite an indecent rapidity; they treat my modest hints for their instruction as so much verbiage, and myself as a mere convenient channel for the publication of their lucubrations. 'You talk of a genuine literary talent being always appreciated by editors,' they write (if not in so many words by implication); 'well, here is an admirable specimen of it (enclosed), and if your remarks are worth a farthing you will get it published for us, somewhere or another, *instanter*, and hand us over the cheque for it. Nor are even these the most unreasonable of my correspondents; for a few, with many acknowledgments for my kindness in having provided a lucrative profession for them, announce their intention of throwing up their present less congenial callings, and coming up to London (one very literally from the Land's End) to live upon it, or, that failing (as there is considerable reason to expect it will), upon *me*.

With some of these correspondents, however, it is impossible (independent of their needs) not to feel an earnest sympathy; they have evidently not only aspirations, but considerable mental gifts, though these have unhappily been cultivated to such little purpose for the object they have in view that they might almost as well have been left untilled. In spite of what I ventured to urge respecting the advantage of knowing 'science, history, politics, English literature, and the art of composition,' they 'don't see why' they shouldn't get on without them. Especially with those who aspire to write fiction (which, by its intrinsic attractiveness no less than by the promise it affords of golden grain, tempts the majority), it is quite pitiful to note how they cling to that notion of 'the corn-sieve,' and cannot be persuaded that story-telling requires an apprenticeship like any other calling. They flatter themselves that they can weave plots as the spider spins his thread from (what let us delicately term) his inner consciousness, and fondly hope that intuition will supply the place of experience. Some of them, with a simplicity that recalls the days of Dick Whittington, think that 'coming up to London' is the essential step to this line of business, as though the provinces contained no fellow-creatures worthy to be depicted by their pen, or as though, in the metropolis, Society would at once exhibit itself to them without concealment, as fashionable beauties bare themselves to the photographers.

This is, of course, the laughable side of the affair, but, to me at least, it has also a serious one; for, to my considerable embarrassment and distress, I find that my well-meaning attempt to point out the advantages of literature as a profession has received a much too free translation, and implanted in many minds hopes that are not only sanguine but Utopian.

For what was written in the essay alluded to I have nothing to reproach myself with, for I told no more than the truth. Nor does the unsettlement of certain young gentleman's futures (since by their own showing they were to the last degree unstable to begin with) affect me so much as their parents and guardians appear to expect; but I am sorry to have shaken however undesignedly, the 'pillars of domestic peace' in any case, and desirous to make all the reparation in my power. I regret most heartily that I am unable to place all literary aspirants in places of emolument and permanency out of hand; but really (with the exception perhaps of the Universal Provider in Westbourne Grove) this is hardly to be expected of any man. The gentleman who raised the devil, and was compelled to furnish occupation for him, affords in fact the only appropriate parallel to my unhappy case. 'If you can do nothing to provide my son with another place,' writes one indignant Paterfamilias, 'at least you owe it to him' (as if I, and not Nature herself, had made the lad dissatisfied with his high stool in a solicitor's office!) 'to give him some practical hints by which he may become a successful writer of fiction.'

One would really think that this individual imagined story-telling to be a sort of sleight-of-hand trick, and that all that is necessary to the attainment of the art is to learn 'how it's done.' I should not like to say that I have known any members of my own profession who are 'no conjurors,' but it is certainly not by conjuring that they have succeeded in it.

'You talk of the art of composition,' writes, on the other hand, another angry correspondent, 'as though it were one of the exact sciences; you might just as well advise your "clever Jack" to study the art of playing the violin.' So that one portion of the public appears to consider the calling of literature mechanical, while another holds it to be a soft of divine instinct!

Since the interest in this subject proves to be so wide-spread, I trust it will not be thought presumptuous in me to offer my own humble experience in this matter for what it is worth. To the public at large a card of admission to my poor manufactory of fiction—a 'very one-horse affair,' as an American gentleman, with whom I had a little difficulty concerning copyright, once described it—may not afford the same satisfaction as a ticket for the private view of the Royal Academy; but the stings of conscience urge me to make to Paterfamilias what amends in the way of 'practical hints' lie in my power, for the wrong I have done to his offspring; and I therefore venture to address to those whom it may concern, and to those only, a few words on the Art of Story-telling.

The chief essential for this line of business, yet one that is much disregarded by many young writers, is the having a story to tell. It is a common supposition that the story will come if you only sit down with a pen in your hand and wait long enough—a parallel case to that which assigns one cow's tail as the measure of distance between this planet and the moon. It is no use 'throwing off' a few brilliant ideas at the commencement, if they are only to be 'passages that lead to nothing;' you must have distinctly in your mind at first what you intend to say at last. 'Let it be granted,' says a great writer (though not one distinguished in fiction), 'that a straight line be drawn from any one point to any other point;' only you must have the 'other point' to begin with, or you can't draw the line. So far from being 'straight,' it goes wabbling aimlessly about like a wire fastened at one end and not at the other, which may dazzle, but cannot sustain; or rather what it does sustain is so exceedingly minute, that it reminds one of the minnow which the inexperienced angler flatters himself he has caught, but which the fisherman has in fact previously put on his hook for bait.

This class of writer is not altogether unconscious of the absence of dramatic interest in his composition. He writes to his editor (I have read a thousand such letters): 'It has been my aim, in the enclosed contribution, to steer clear of the faults of the sensational school of fiction, and I have designedly abstained from stimulating the unwholesome taste for excitement.' In which high moral purpose he has undoubtedly succeeded; but, unhappily, in nothing else. It is quite true that some writers of fiction neglect 'story' almost entirely, but then they are perhaps the greatest writers of all. Their genius is so transcendent that they can afford to dispense with 'plot;' their humour, their pathos, and their delineation of human nature are amply sufficient, without any such meretricious attraction; whereas our too ambitious young friend is in the position of the needy knife-grinder, who has not only no story to tell, but in lieu of it only holds up his coat and breeches 'torn in the scuffle'—the evidence of his desperate and ineffectual struggles with literary composition. I have known such an aspirant to instance Miss Gaskell's 'Cranford' as a parallel to the backboneless flesh-and-bloodless creation of his own immature fancy, and to recommend the acceptance of the latter upon the ground of their common rejection of startling plot and dramatic situation. The two compositions have certainly *that* in common; and the flawless diamond has some things, such as mere sharpness and smoothness, in common with the broken beer-bottle.

Many young authors of the class I have in my mind, while more modest as respects their own merits, are even still less so as regards their expectations from others. 'If you will kindly furnish me with a subject,' so runs a letter now before me, 'I am sure I could do very well; my difficulty is that I never can think of anything to write about. Would you be so good as to oblige me with a plot for a novel?' It would have been infinitely more reasonable of course, and much cheaper, for me to grant it, if the applicant had made a request for my watch and chain;[6] but the marvel is that folks should feel any attraction towards a calling for which Nature has denied them even the raw materials. It is true that there are some great talkers who have manifestly nothing to say, but they don't ask their hearers to supply them with a topic of conversation in order to be set agoing.

[6] To compare small things with great, I remember Sir Walter Scott being thus applied to for some philanthropic object. 'Money,' said the applicant, who had some part proprietorship in a literary miscellany, 'I don't ask for, since I know you have many claims upon your purse; but would you write us a little paper gratuitously for the "Keepsake"?'

'My great difficulty,' the would-be writer of fiction often says, 'is how to begin;' whereas in fact the difficulty arises rather from his not knowing how to end. Before undertaking the management of a train, however short, it is absolutely necessary to know its destination. Nothing is more common than to hear it said that an author 'does not know where to stop;' but how much more deplorable is the position of the passengers when there is no terminus whatsoever! They feel their carriage 'slowing,' and put their heads expectantly out of window, but there is no platform—no station. When they took their tickets, they understood that they were 'booked through' to the *dénouement*, and certainly had no idea of having been brought so far merely to admire the scenery, for which only a very few care the least about.

As a rule, anyone who can tell a good story can write one, so there really need be no mistake about his qualification; such a man will be careful not to be wearisome, and to keep his point, or his catastrophe, well in hand. Only, in writing, there is necessarily greater art. *There* expansion is of course absolutely necessary; but this is not to be done, like spreading gold leaf, by flattening out good material. *That* is 'padding,' a device as dangerous as it is unworthy; it is much better to make your story a pollard—to cut it down to a mere anecdote—than to get it lost in a forest of verbiage. No line of it, however seemingly discursive, should be aimless, but should have some relation to the matter in hand; and if you find the story interesting to yourself notwithstanding that you know the end of it, it will certainly interest the reader.

The manner in which a good story grows under the hand is so remarkable, that no tropic vegetation can show the like of it. For, consider, when you have got your germ—the mere idea, not half a dozen lines perhaps—which is to form your plot, how small a thing it is compared with, say, the thousand pages which it has to occupy in the three-volume novel! Yet to the story-teller the germ is everything. When I was a very young man—a quarter of a century ago, alas!—and had very little experience in these matters, I was reading on a coachbox (for I read everywhere in those days) an account of some gigantic trees; one of them was described as sound outside, but within, for many feet, a mass of rottenness and decay. If a boy should climb up birdsnesting into the fork of it, thought I, he might go down feet first and hands overhead, and never be heard of again. How inexplicable too, as well as melancholy, such a disappearance would be!

Then, 'as when a great thought strikes along the brain and flushes all the cheek,' it struck me what an appropriate end it would be—with fear (lest he should turn up again) instead of hope for the fulcrum to move the reader—for a bad character of a novel. Before I had left the coachbox I had thought out 'Lost Sir Massingberd.'

The character was drawn from life, but unfortunately from hearsay; he had flourished—to the great terror of his neighbours—two generations before me, so that I had to be indebted to others for his portraiture, which was a great disadvantage. It was necessary that the lost man should be an immense scoundrel to prevent pity being excited by the catastrophe, and at that time I did not know any very wicked people. The book was a successful one, but it needs no critic to point out how much better the story might have been told. The interest in the gentleman, buried upright in his oak coffin, is inartistically weakened by other sources of excitement; like an extravagant cook, the young author is apt to be too lavish with his materials, and in after days, when the larder is more difficult to fill, he bitterly regrets it. The representation of a past time I also found it very difficult to compass, and I am convinced that for any writer to attempt such a thing, when he can avoid it, is an error in judgment. The author who undertakes to resuscitate and clothe with flesh and blood the dry bones of his ancestors, has indeed this advantage, that, however unlifelike his characters may be, there is no one in a position to prove it; it is not 'a difference of opinion between himself and twelve of his fellow-countrymen,' or a matter on which he can be condemned by overwhelming evidence; but, on the other hand, he creates for himself unnecessary difficulties. I will add, for the benefit of those literary aspirants to whom these remarks are especially addressed—a circumstance which, I hope, will be taken as an excuse for the writing of my own affairs at all, which would otherwise be an unpardonable presumption—that these difficulties are not the worst of it; for when the novel founded on the Past has been written, it will not be read by a tenth of those who would read it if it were a novel of the Present.

Even at the date I speak of, however, I was not so young as to attempt to create the characters of a story out of my own imagination, and I believe that the whole of its *dramatis personæ* (except the chief personage) were taken from the circle of my own acquaintance. This is a matter, by-the-bye, on which considerable judgment and good taste have to be exercised; for if the likeness of the person depicted is recognisable by his friends (he never recognises it by any chance himself), or still more by his enemies, it is no longer a sketch from life, but a lampoon. It will naturally be asked by some: 'But if you draw the man to the life, how can he fail to be known?' For this there is the simplest remedy. You describe his character, but under another skin; if he is tall you make him short, if dark, fair; or you make such alterations in his circumstances as shall prevent identification, while retaining them to a sufficient extent to influence his behaviour. In the framework which most (though not all) skilled workmen draw of their stories before they begin to furnish them with so much even as a door-mat, the real name of each individual to be described should be placed (as a mere aid to memory) by the side of that under which he appears in the drama; and I would strongly recommend the builder to write his real names in cipher; for I have known at least one instance in which the entire list of the *dramatis personæ* of a novel was carried off by a person more curious than conscientious, and afterwards revealed to those concerned—a circumstance which, though it increased the circulation of the story, did not add to the personal popularity of the author.

If a story-teller is prolific, the danger of his characters coinciding with those of people in real life who are unknown to him is much greater than would be imagined; the mere similarity of name may of course be disregarded; but when in addition to that there is also a resemblance of circumstance, it is difficult to persuade the man of flesh and blood that his portrait is an undesigned one. The author of 'Vanity Fair' fell, in at least one instance, into a most unfortunate mistake of this kind; while a not less popular author even gave his hero the same name and place in the Ministry which were (subsequently) possessed by a living politician.

It is better, however, for his own reputation that the story-teller should risk a few actions for libel on account of these unfortunate coincidences than that he should adopt the melancholy device of using blanks or asterisks. With the minor novelists of a quarter of a century ago it was quite common to introduce their characters as Mr. A and Mr. B, and very difficult their readers found it to interest themselves in the fortunes and misfortunes of an initial:

It was in the summer of the year 18—, and the sun was setting behind the low western hills beneath which stands the town of C; its dying gleams glistened on the weather-cock of the little church, beneath whose tower two figures were standing, so deep in shadow that little more could be made out concerning them save that they were young persons of the opposite sex. The elder and taller, however, was the fascinating Lord B; the younger (presenting a strong contrast to her companion in social position, but yet belonging to the true nobility of nature) was no other than the beautiful Patty G, the cobbler's daughter.

This style of narrative should be avoided.

Another difficulty of the story-teller, and one unhappily in which no advice can be of much service to him, is how to describe the lapse of time and of locomotion. To the dramatist nothing is easier than to print in the middle of his playbill, 'Forty years are here supposed to have elapsed;' or 'Scene I.: A drawing-room in Mayfair; Scene II.: Greenland.' But the story-teller has to describe how these little changes are effected, without being able to take his readers into his confidence.[7] He can't say, 'Gentle reader, please to imagine that the winter is over, and the summer has come round since the conclusion of our last chapter.' Curiously enough, however, the lapse of years is far easier to suggest than that of hours; and locomotion from Islington to India than the act, for instance, of leaving the room. If passion enters into the scene, and your heroine can be represented as banging the door behind her, and bringing down the plaster from the ceiling, the thing is easy enough, and may be even made a dramatic incident; but to describe, without baldness, Jones rising from the tea-table and taking his departure in cold blood, is a much more difficult business than you may imagine. When John the footman has to enter and interrupt a conversation on the stage, the audience see him come and go, and think nothing of it; but to inform the reader of your novel of a similar incident—and especially of John's going—without spoiling the whole scene by the introduction of the commonplace, requires (let me tell you) the touch of a master.

[7] That last, indeed, is a thing which, with all deference to some great names in fiction, should in my judgment never be done. It is hard enough for him as it is to simulate real life, without the poor showman's reaching out from behind the curtain to shake hands with his audience.

When you have got the outline of your plot, and the characters that seem appropriate to play in it, you turn to that so-called 'commonplace book,' in which, if you know your trade, you will have set down anything noteworthy and illustrative of human nature that has come under your notice, and single out such instances as are most fitting; and finally you will select your scene (or the opening one) in which your drama is to be played. And here I may say, that while it is indispensable that the persons represented should be familiar to you, it is not necessary that the places should be; you should have visited them, of course, in person, but it is my experience that for a description of the salient features of any locality the less you stay there the better. The man who has lived in Switzerland all his life can never describe it (to the outsider) so graphically as the (intelligent) tourist; just as the man who has science at his fingers' ends does not succeed so well as the man with whom science has not yet become second nature, in making an abstruse subject popular.

Nor is it to be supposed that a story with very accurate local colouring cannot be written, the scenes of which are placed in a country which the writer has never beheld. This requires, of course, both study and judgment, but it can be done so as to deceive, if not the native, at least the

Englishman who has himself resided there. I never yet knew an Australian who could be persuaded that the author of 'Never Too Late to Mend' had not visited the underworld, or a sailor that he who wrote 'Hard Cash' had never been to sea. The fact is, information, concerning which dull folks make so much fuss, can be attained by anybody who chooses to spend his time that way; and by persons of intelligence (who are not so solicitous to know how blacking is made) can be turned, in a manner not dreamt of by cram-coaches, to really good account.

The general impression perhaps conveyed by the above remarks will be that to those who go to work in the manner described—for many writers of course have quite other processes—story-telling must be a mechanical trade. Yet nothing can be farther from the fact. These preliminary arrangements have the effect of so steeping the mind in the subject in hand, that when the author begins his work he is already in a world apart from his everyday one; the characters of his story people it; and the events that occur to them are as material, so far as the writer is concerned, as though they happened under his roof. Indeed, it is a question for the metaphysician whether the professional story-teller has not a shorter lease of life than his fellow-creatures, since, in addition to his hours of sleep (of which he ought by rights to have much more than the usual proportion), he passes a large part of his sentient being outside the pale of ordinary existence. The reference to sleep 'by rights' may possibly suggest to the profane that the storyteller has a claim to it on the ground of having induced slumber in his fellow-creatures; but my meaning is that the mental wear and tear caused by work of this kind is infinitely greater than that produced by mere application even to abstruse studies (as any doctor will witness), and requires a proportionate degree of recuperation.

I do not pretend to quote the experience (any more than the mode of composition) of other writers—though with that of most of my brethren and superiors in the craft I am well acquainted—but I am convinced that to work the brain at night in the way of imagination is little short of an act of suicide. Dr. Treichler's recent warnings upon this subject are startling enough, even as addressed to students, but in their application to poets and novelists they have far greater significance. It may be said that journalists (whose writings, it is whispered, have a close connection with fiction) always write in the 'small hours,' but their mode of life is more or less shaped to meet their exceptional requirements; whereas we storytellers live like other people (only more purely), and if we consume the midnight oil, use perforce another system of illumination also—we burn the candle at both ends. A great novelist who adopted this baneful practice and indirectly lost his life by it (through insomnia) notes what is very curious, that notwithstanding his mind was so occupied, when awake, with the creatures of his imagination, he never dreamt of them; which I think is also the general experience. But he does not tell us for how many hours *before* he went to sleep, and tossed upon his restless pillow till far into the morning, he was unable to get rid of those whom his enchanter's wand had summoned.[8] What is even more curious than the story-teller's never dreaming of the shadowy beings who engross so much of his thoughts, is that (so far as my own experience goes at least) when a story is once written and done with, no matter how forcibly it may have interested and excited the writer during its progress, it fades almost instantly from the mind, and leaves, by some benevolent arrangement of nature, a *tabula rasa*—a blank space for the next one. Everyone must recollect that anecdote of Walter Scott, who, on hearing one of his own poems ('My hawk is tired of perch and hood') sung in a London drawing-room, observed with innocent approbation, 'Byron's, of course;' and so it is with us lesser folks. A very humorous sketch might be given (and it would not be overdrawn) of some prolific novelist getting hold, under some strange roof, of the 'library edition' of his own stories, and perusing them with great satisfaction and many appreciative ejaculations, such as 'Now this *is* good;' 'I wonder how it will end;' or 'George Eliot's, *of course*!

[8] Speaking of dreams, the composition of Khubla Khan and of one or two other literary fragments during sleep has led to the belief that dreams are often useful to the writer of fiction; but in my own case, at least, I can recall but a single instance of it, nor have I ever heard of their doing one pennyworth of good to any of my contemporaries.

Although a good allowance of sleep is absolutely necessary for imaginative brain work, long holidays are not so. I have noticed that those who let their brains 'lie fallow,' as it is termed, for any considerable time, are by no means the better for it; but, on the other hand, some daily recreation, by which a genuine interest is excited and maintained, is almost indispensable. It is no use to 'take up a book,' and far less to attempt 'to refresh the machine,' as poor Sir Walter did, by trying another kind of composition; what is needed is an altogether new object for the intellectual energies, by which, though they are stimulated, they shall not be strained.

Advice such as I have ventured to offer may seem 'to the general' of small importance, but to those I am especially addressing it is worthy of their attention, if only as the result of a personal experience unusually prolonged; and I have nothing unfortunately but advice to offer. To the question addressed to me with such *naïveté* by so many correspondents, 'How do you make your plots?' (as if they were consulting the Cook's Oracle), I can return no answer. I don't know, myself; they are sometimes suggested by what I hear or read, but more commonly they suggest themselves unsought.

I once heard two popular story-tellers, A who writes seldom, but with much ingenuity of construction, and B who is very prolific in pictures of everyday life, discoursing on this subject.

'Your fecundity,' said A, 'astounds me; I can't think where you get your plots from.'

'Plots?' replied B; 'oh! I don't trouble myself about *them*. To tell you the truth, I generally take a bit of one of yours, which is amply sufficient for my purpose.'

This was very wrong of B; and it is needless to say I do not quote his system for imitation. A man should tell his own story without plagiarism. As to Truth being stranger than Fiction, that is all nonsense; it is a proverb set about by Nature to conceal her own want of originality. I am not like that pessimist philosopher who assumed her malignity from the fact of the obliquity of the ecliptic; but the truth is, Nature is a pirate. She has not hesitated to plagiarise from even so humble an individual as myself. Years after I had placed my wicked baronet in his living tomb, she starved to death a hunter in Mexico under precisely similar circumstances; and so late as last month she has done the same in a forest in Styria. Nay, on my having found occasion in a certain story ('a small thing, but my own') to get rid of the whole wicked population of an island by suddenly submerging it in the sea, what did Nature do? She waited for an insultingly short time (if her idea was that the story would be forgotten), and then reproduced the same circumstances on her own account (and without the least acknowledgment) in the Indian seas. My attention was drawn to both these breaches of copyright by several correspondents, but I had no redress, the offender being beyond the jurisdiction of the Court of Chancery.

When the story-teller has finished his task and surmounted every obstacle to his own satisfaction, he has still a difficulty to face in the choice of a title. He may invent indeed an eminently appropriate one, but it is by no means certain he will be allowed to keep it. Of course he has done his best to steer clear of that borne by any other novel; but among the thousands that have been brought out within the last forty years, and which have been forgotten even if they were ever known, how can he know whether the same name has not been hit upon? He goes to Stationers' Hall to make inquiries; but—mark the usefulness of that institution—he finds that books are only entered there under their authors' names. His search is therefore necessarily futile, and he has to publish his story under the apprehension (only too well founded, as I have good cause to know) that the High Court of Chancery will prohibit its sale upon the ground of infringement of title.

PENNY FICTION

It is now nearly a quarter of a century ago since a popular novelist revealed to the world in a well-known periodical the existence of the 'Unknown Public;' and a very curious revelation it was. He showed us that the few thousands of persons who had hitherto imagined themselves to be the public—so far, at least, as their being the arbiters of popularity in respect to writers of fiction was concerned—were in fact nothing of the kind; that the subscribers to the circulating libraries, the members of book clubs, the purchasers of magazines and railway novels, might indeed have their favourites, but that these last were 'nowhere,' as respected the number of their backers, in comparison with novelists whose names and works appear in penny journals and nowhere else.

This class of literature was of considerable dimensions even in the days when Mr. Wilkie Collins first called attention to it; but the luxuriance of its growth has since become tropical. His observations are drawn from some half a dozen specimens of it only, whereas I now hold in my hand—or rather in both hands— nearly half a hundred of them. The population of readers must be dense indeed in more than one sense that can support such a crop.

Doubtless the individual circulation of none of these serials is equal to that of the most successful of them at the date of their first discovery; but those who read them must, from various causes, of which the most obvious is the least important, have trebled in number. Population, that is to say, has increased in very small proportion as compared with the increase of those who very literally run and read—the peripatetic students, who study on their way to work or even as they work, including, I am sorry to say, the telegraph boy on his errand.

Nevertheless, notwithstanding its gigantic dimensions, the Unknown Public remains practically as unknown as ever. The literary wares that find such favour with it do not meet the eye of the ordinary observer. They are to be found neither at the bookseller's nor on the railway stall. But in back streets, in small dark shops, in the company of cheap tobacco, hardbake (and, at the proper season, valentines), their leaves lie thick as those in Vallombrosa. Early in the week is their springtime, when they are put forth from Heaven knows what printing-houses in courts and alleys, to lie for a few days only on the counter in huge piles. On Saturdays, albeit that is their nominal publishing day, they have for the most part disappeared. For this sort of literature has one decidedly advanced feature, and possesses one virtue of endurance—it comes out ever so long before the date it bears upon its title-page, and 'when the world shall have passed away' will, by a few days at least, if faith is to be placed in figures, survive it.

Why it should have any date at all no man can tell. There is nothing in the contents that is peculiar to one year—or, to say truth, of one era—rather than another. As a rule, indeed, time and space are alike annihilated in them, in order to make two lovers happy. The general terms in which they are written is one of their peculiar features. One would think that, instead of being as unlike real life as stories professing to deal with it can be, they were photographs of it, and that the writers, as in the following instance, had always the fear of the law of libel before their eyes:

We must now request our readers to accompany us into an obscure *cul de sac* opening into a narrow street branching off Holborn. For many reasons we do not choose to be more precise as to locality.

Of course in this *cul de sac* is a Private Inquiry Office, with a detective in it. But in defining even him the novelist gives himself no trouble to arouse excitement in his readers: they have paid their penny for the history of this interesting person, and, that being done, they may read about him or not, as they please. One would really think that the author of the story was also the proprietor of the periodical.

Those who desire (he says) to make the acquaintance of this somewhat remarkable person have only to step with us into the little dusky room where he is seated, and we shall have much pleasure in introducing him to their notice.

—A sentence which has certainly the air of saying, 'You may be introduced to him, or you may let it alone.'

The coolness with which everything is said and done in penny fiction is indeed most remarkable, and should greatly recommend it to that respectable class who have a horror of 'sensation.' In a story, for example, that purports to describe University life (and is as much like it as the camel produced from the German professor's self-consciousness must have been to a real camel) there is an underplot of an amazing kind. The wicked undergraduate, notwithstanding that he has the advantage of being a baronet, is foiled in his attempt to win the affections of a young woman in humble life, and the virtuous hero of the story recommends her to the consideration of his negro servant:

'Talk to her, Monday,' whispered Jack, 'and see if she loves you.'

For a short time Monday and Ada were in close conversation.

Then Monday uttered a cry like a war-whoop.

'It am come all right, sare. Missy Ada says she not really care for Sir Sydney, and she will be my little wife,' he said.

'I congratulate you, Monday,' answered Jack.

In half an hour more they arrived at the house of John Radford, plumber and glazier, who was Ada's father.

Mr. and Mrs. Radford and their two sons received their daughter and her companions with that unstudied civility which contrasts so favourably with the stuck-up ceremony of many in a higher position. They were not prejudiced against Monday on account of his dark skin.

It was enough for them that he was the man of Ada's choice.

Mrs. Radford even went so far as to say, 'Well, for a coloured gentleman, he is very handsome and quite nice mannered, though I think Ada's been a little sly in telling us nothing about her engagement to the last.'

They did not know all.

Nor was it advisable that they should.

Still they knew something—for example, that their new son-in-law was a black man, which one would have thought might have struck them as phenomenal. They take it, however, quite quietly and as a matter of course. Now, surely, even among plumbers and glaziers, it must be thought as strange for one's daughter to marry a black man as a lord. Yet, out of this dramatic situation the author makes nothing at all, but treats it as coolly as his *dramatis personæ* do themselves. Now *my* notion would have been to make the bridegroom a black lord, and then to portray, with admirable skill, the conflicting emotions of his mother-in-law, disgusted on the one hand by his colour, attracted on the other by his rank. But 'sensation' is evidently out of the line of the penny novelist: he gives his facts, which are certainly remarkable, then leaves both his characters and his readers to draw their own conclusions.

The total absence of local scenery from these half hundred romances is also curious, and becomes so very marked when the novelists are so imprudent as to take their *dramatis personæ* out of England, that one can't help wondering whether these gentlemen have ever been in foreign parts themselves, or even read about them. Here is the conclusion of a romance which leaves nothing to be desired in the way of brevity, but is unquestionably a little abrupt and vague:

A year has passed away, and we are far from England and the English climate.

Whither 'we' have gone the author does not say, nor even indicate the hemisphere. It will be imagined, perhaps, that we shall find out where we are by the indication of the flora and fauna.

A lady and gentleman before the dawn of day have been climbing up an arid road in the direction of a dark ridge.

Observe, again, the ingenious vagueness of the description: an 'arid road' which may mean Siberia, and a 'dark ridge' which may mean the Himalayas.

The dawn suddenly comes upon them in all its glory. Birds twittered in their willow gorges, and it was a very glorious day. Arthur and Emily had passed the night at the ranche, and he had now taken her up to look at the mine which at all events had introduced them. He had previously taken her to see his mother's grave, the mother whom he had so loved. The mine after some delay proved more prosperous than ever. It was not sold, but is the 'appanage' of the younger sons of the house of Dacres.

With the exception of the 'ranche,' it will be remarked that there is not one word in the foregoing description to fix locality. The mine and the ranche together seem indeed to suggest South America. But—I ask for information—do birds twitter there in willow gorges? Younger sons of noble families proverbially come off second best in this country, but if one of them found his only 'appanage' was a mine, he would surely with some justice make a remonstrance.

The readers of this class of fiction will not have Dumas at any price—or, at all events, not at a penny. Mr. Collins tells us how 'Monte Christo' was once spread before them, and how they turned from that gorgeous feast with indifference, and fell back upon their tripe and onions—their nameless authors. But some of those who write for them have adopted one peculiarity of Dumas. The short jerky sentences which disfigure the 'Three Musketeers,' and indeed all that great novelist's works, are very frequent with them, which induces me to believe that they are paid by the line.

On the other hand, some affect fashionable description and conversation which are drawn out in 'passages that lead to nothing' of an amazing length.

'Where have I been,' replied Clyde with a carelessness which was half forced 'Oh, I have been over to Higham to see the dame.'

'Ah, yes,' said Sir Edward, 'and how is the poor old creature?'

'Quite well,' said Clyde, as he sat down and took up the menu of the elaborate dinner. 'Quite well, she sent her best respects,' he added, but he said nothing of the lodger, pretty Miss Mary Westlake.

And when, a moment afterwards, the door opened and Grace came flowing in with her lithe noiseless step, dressed in one of Worth's masterpieces, a wonder of amber, satin, and antique lace, he raised his eyes and looked at her with an earnest scrutiny—so earnest that she paused with her hand on his chair, and met his eyes with a questioning glance.

'Do you like my new dress?' she said with a calm smile.

'Your dress?' he said. 'Yes, yes, it is very pretty, very.' But to himself he added, 'Yes, they are alike, strangely alike.'

Which last remark may be applied with justice to the conversations of all our novelists. There appears no necessity for their commencement, no reason for their continuance, no object in their conclusion; the reader finds himself in a forest of verbiage from which he is extricated only at the end of the chapter, which is always, however, 'to be continued.'

It is true that these story-tellers for the million generally keep 'a gallop for the avenue' (an incident of a more or less exciting kind to finish up with), but it is so brief and unsatisfactory that it hardly rises to a canter; the author never seems to get into his stride. The following is a fair example:

But before we let the curtain fall, we must glance for a moment at another picture—a sad and painful one. In one of those retreats, worse than a living tomb, where reside those whose reason is dead, though their bodies still live, is a small spare cell. The sole occupant is a woman, young and very beautiful. Sometimes she is quiet and gentle as a child; sometimes her fits of frenzy are frightful to witness; but the only word she utters is 'Revenge,' and on her hand she always wears a plain gold band with a cross of black pearls.

This conclusion, which I chanced upon before I read the tale which preceded it, naturally interested me immensely. Here, thought I, is at last an exciting story; I shall now find one of those literary prizes in hopes, perhaps, of hitting upon which the penny public endures so many blanks. I was quite prepared to have my blood curdled; my lips were ready for a full draught of gore; yet, I give you my word, there was nothing in the whole story worse than a bankruptcy.

This is what makes the success of penny fiction so remarkable; there is nothing whatever in the way of dramatic interest to account for it; nor of impropriety either. Like the lady friend of Dr. Johnson, who congratulated him that there were no improper words in his dictionary, and received from that unconciliatory sage the reply, 'You have been looking for them, have you?' I have carefully searched my fifty samples of penny fiction for something wrong, and have not found it. It is as pure as milk, or, at all events, as milk-and-water. Unlike the Minerva Press, too, it does not deal with eminent persons: wicked peers are rare; fraud is usually confined within what may be called its natural limits—the lawyer's office; the attention paid to the heroines not only by their heroes, but by their unsuccessful and objectionable rivals, is generally of the most honourable kind; and platitude and dulness hold undisputed sway.

In one or two of these periodicals there is indeed an example of the mediaeval melodrama; but 'Ralpho the Mysterious' is by no means thrilling. Indeed, when I remember that 'Ivanhoe' was once published in a penny journal and proved a total failure, and then contemplate the popularity of 'Ralpho,' I am more at sea as to what it is that attracts the million than ever.

'Noble youth,' cried the King as he embraced Ralpho, 'to you we must entrust the training of our cavalry. I hold here the list which has been made out of the troops which will come at the signal. To certain of our nobles we have entrusted certain of our *corps d'armée*, but unto you, Ralpho, we must entrust our horse, for in that service you can display that wonderful dexterity with the sword which has made your name so famous.'

'Sire,' cried our hero, as he dropped on one knee and took the King's hand, pressing it to his lips, 'thou hast indeed honoured me by such a reward, but I cannot accept it.'

'How!' cried the King; 'hast thou so soon tired of my service?'

'Not so, sire. To serve you I would shed the last drop of my blood. But if I were to accept this command, I should cease to do the service for the cause which now it has pleased you to say I have done. No, sire, let me remain the guardian of my King—his secret agent. I, with my sword alone, will defend my country and my King.'

'Be not rash, Ralpho; already hast thou done more than any man ever did before. Run no more danger.'

'Sire, if I have served you, grant my request. Let it be as I have said.'

'It shall be so, mysterious youth. Thou shalt be my secret agent. Take this ring, and wear it for my sake; and, hark ye, gentlemen, when Ralpho shows that ring, obey him as if he were ourselves.'

'We will,' cried the nobles.

Then the King took the Star of St. Stanislaus, and fixed it on our hero's breast.

Now, to my mind, though his preferring to be 'a secret agent' to becoming a generalissimo of the Polish cavalry is as modest as it is original, Ralpho is too 'goody-goody' to be called 'the Mysterious.' He reminds me, too, in his way of mixing chivalry with self-interest, of those enterprising officers in fighting regiments who send in applications for their own V.C.s while their comrades remain in modest expectation of them.

I am inclined to think, however, from the following advertisement, that some author has been recently piling up the virtues of his hero too strongly for the very delicate stomachs of the penny public, who, it is evident, resent superlatives of all kinds, and are commonplace and conventional to the marrow of their bones: 'T.B. TIMMINS is informed that he cannot be promised another story like "Mandragora," since, in deciding the contents of our journal, the tastes of readers have to be considered whose interest cannot be aroused by the impossible deeds of impossible creatures.' Alas! I wish from my heart I knew what 'deeds' or 'creatures' *do* arouse the interest of this (to me) inexplicable public; for though I have before me the stories they obviously take delight in, why they do so I cannot tell.

At the 'Answers to Correspondents,' indeed, which form a leading feature in most of these penny journals, one may exclaim, with the colonel in 'Woodstock,' when, after many ghosts, he grapples with Wildrake: 'Thou at least art palpable.' Here we have the real readers, asking questions upon matters that concern them, and from these we shall surely get at the back of their minds. But it is unfortunately not so certain that these 'Answers to Correspondents' are not themselves fictions, like all the rest—only invented by the editor instead of the author, and coming in handy to fill up a vacant page. It is, to my mind, incredible that a public so every way different from that of the Mechanic's Institute, and to whom mere information is likely to be anything but attractive, should be genuinely solicitous to learn that 'Needles were first made in England in Cheapside, in the reign of Queen Mary, by a negro from Spain;' or that 'The family name of the Duke of Norfolk is Howard, although the younger members of it call themselves Talbot.'

Even the remonstrance of 'Our Correspondence Editor' with a gentleman who wishes to learn 'How to manufacture dynamite' seems to me artificial; as though the idea of saying a few words in season against explosive compounds had occurred to him, without any particular opportunity having really offered itself for the expression of his views.

There are, however, one or two advertisements decidedly genuine, and which prove that the readers of penny fiction are not so immersed in romance but that they have their eyes open to the main chance and their material responsibilities. 'ANXIOUS TO KNOW,' for example, is informed that 'The widow, unless otherwise decreed, keeps possession of furniture on her marriage, and the daughter cannot claim it;' while SKIBBS is assured that 'After such a lapse of time there will be no danger of a warrant being issued for leaving his wife and family chargeable to the parish.'

As when Mr. Wilkie Collins made his first voyage of discovery into these unknown latitudes, the penny journals are largely used for forming matrimonial engagements, and for adjudicating upon all questions of propriety in connection with the affections. 'It is just bordering on folly,' 'NANCY BLAKE' is informed, 'to marry a man six years your junior.' In answer to an inquiry from 'LOVING OLIVIA' whether 'an engaged gentleman is at liberty to go to a theatre without taking his young lady with him,' she is told 'Yes; but we imagine he would not often do so.'

Some tender questions are mixed up with others of a more practical sort. 'LADY HILDA' is informed that 'it is very seldom children are born healthy whose father has married before he is three-and-twenty; that long engagements are not only unnecessary but injurious; and that washing the head will remove the scurf.' 'LEONE' is assured that 'it is not necessary to be married in two churches, one being quite sufficient;' that 'there is no truth in the saying that it is unlucky to marry a person of the same complexion;' and that 'a gentle aperient will remove nettle-rash.'

'VIRGINIE' (who, by the way, should surely be VIRGINIUS) is thus tenderly sympathised with:

'It does seem rather hard that you should be deprived of all opportunity of having a *tête-à-tête* with your betrothed, owing to her being obliged to entertain other company, although there are others of the family who can do so; still, as her mother insists upon it, and will not let you enjoy the society of her daughter uninterrupted, you might resort to a little harmless strategy, and whenever your stated evenings for calling are broken in on that way, ask the young lady to take a walk with you, or go to a place of amusement. She can then excuse herself to her friends without a breach of etiquette, and you can enjoy your *tête-à-tête* undisturbed.'

The photographs of lady correspondents which are received by the editors of most of these journals are apparently very numerous, and, if we may believe their description of them, all ravishingly beautiful. It is no wonder they receive many applications of the following nature:

'CLYDE, a rising young doctor, twenty-two, fair, with a nice house and servants; being tired of bachelor life, wishes to receive the carte-de-visite of a dark, fascinating young lady, of from seventeen to twenty years of age; no money essential, but good birth indispensable. She must be fond of music and children, and very loving and affectionate.'

Another doctor:

'Twenty-nine, of a loving and amiable disposition, and who has at present an income of £120 a year, is desirous to make an immediate engagement with a lady about his own age, who must be possessed of a little money, so that by their united efforts he may soon become a member of a lucrative and honourable profession.'

How the 'united efforts' of two young people, however enthusiastic, can make a man an M.D. or an M.R.C.S. (except that love conquers all things) is more than one can understand. The last advertisement I shall quote affects me nearly, for it is from an eminent member of my own profession:

'ALEXIS, a popular author in the prime of life, of an affectionate disposition, and fond of home, and the extent and pressing nature of whose work have prevented him from mixing much in society, would be glad to correspond with a young lady not above thirty. She must be of a pleasing appearance, amiable, intelligent, and domestic.'

If it is with the readers of penny fiction that Alexis has established his popularity, I would like to know how he did it, and who he is. To discover this last is, however, an impossibility. These novelists all write anonymously, nor do their works ever appear before the public in another guise. There is sometimes a melancholy pretence to the contrary put forth in the 'Answers to Correspondents.' 'PHOENIX,' for example, is informed that 'The story about which he inquires will not be published in book form at the time he mentions.' But the fact is it will never be so published at all. It has been written, like all its congeners, for the unknown millions and for no one else.

Some years ago, in a certain great literary organ, it was stated of one of these penny journals (which has not forgotten to advertise the eulogy) that 'its novels, are equal to the best works of fiction to be got at the circulating libraries.' The critic who so expressed himself must have done so in a moment of hilarity which I trust was not produced by liquor; for 'the best works of fiction to be got at the circulating libraries' obviously include those of George Eliot, Trollope, Reade, Black, and Blackmore, while the novels I am discussing are inferior to the worst. They are as crude and ineffective in their pictures of domestic life as they are deficient in dramatic incident; they are vapid, they are dull. Indeed, the total absence of humour, and even of the least attempt at it, is most remarkable. There is now and then a description of the playing of some practical joke, such as tying two Chinamen's tails together, the effect of the relation of which is melancholy in the extreme, but there is no approach to fun in the whole penny library. And yet it attracts, it is calculated, four millions of readers—a fact which makes my mouth water like that of Tantalus.

When Mr. Wilkie Collins wrote of the Unknown Public it is clear he was still hopeful of them. He thought it 'a question of time' only. 'The largest audience,' he says, 'for periodical literature in this age of periodicals must obey the universal law of progress, and sooner or later learn to discriminate. When that period comes the readers who rank by millions will be the readers who give the widest reputations, who return the richest rewards, and who will therefore command the services of the best writers of their time.' This prophecy has, curiously enough, been fulfilled in a different direction from that anticipated by him who uttered it. The penny papers—that is, the provincial penny newspapers—*do* now, under the syndicate system, command the services of our most eminent novel writers;

but Penny Fiction proper—that is to say, the fiction published in the penny literary journals—is just where it was a quarter of a century ago.

With the opportunity of comparison afforded to its readers one would say this would be impossible, but as a matter of fact, the opportunity is *not* offered. The readers of Penny Fiction do not read newspapers; political events do not interest them, nor even social events, unless they are of the class described in the *Police News*, which, I remark—and the fact is not without significance—does not need to add fiction to its varied attractions.

But who, it will be asked, *are* the public who don't read newspapers, and whose mental calibre is such that they require to be told by a correspondence editor that 'any number over the two thousand will certainly be in the three thousand'?

I believe, though the vendors of the commodity in question profess to be unable to give any information on the matter, that the majority are female domestic servants.

As to what attracts them in their favourite literature, that is a much more knotty question. My own theory is that, just as Mr. Tupper achieved his immense popularity by never going over the heads of his readers, and showing that poetry was, after all, not such a difficult thing to be understood, so the writers of Penny Fiction, in clothing very conventional thoughts in rather high-faluting English, have found the secret of success. Each reader says to himself (or herself), 'That is *my* thought, which I would have myself expressed in those identical words, if I had only known how.

HOTELS.

The desire for cheap holidays—as concerns going a long distance for little money—is no doubt very general, but it is not universal. It demands, like the bicycle, both youth and vigour. In mature years, not only because we are more fastidious, but because we are less robust, the element of cheapness, though always agreeable, is subsidiary to that of comfort. For my own part, if the chance were offered me to travel night and day for forty-eight hours anywhere—though it was to the Elysian Fields—and that in a Pullman car, and for nothing, I would rather go to Southend at my own expense from Saturday to Monday. Suppose the former journey to be commenced by a Channel passage and continued in a third-class carriage, I would rather stop at home. Or if, in addition to the other discomforts, I am to be a unit among 100 excursionists, with a coupon that insures my being lodged on the sixth floor everywhere, I had rather take a month's quiet holiday in London at the House of Detention.

These things are matters of taste; but it is certain that a very large number of people, who, like myself, are neither rich nor in a position which justifies them in giving themselves airs, consider quiet, comfort, and the absence of petty cares the most essential conditions of a holiday. These views necessitate some expense and generally limit the excursions of those who entertain them to their native land; but, on the other hand, they have their advantages. They give one, for example, a great experience in the matter of hotels.

As I idly flutter the yellow leaves of the advertisements of inns in 'Bradshaw,' they call up pictures in my mind quite undreamt of by the proprietors. I have been a sojourner in almost all of these which are described as 'situated in picturesque localities.' They are all—it is in print and must be true—'first-class' hotels; they have most of them 'unrivalled accommodation;' not a few of them have been 'patronised by Royalty,' and one of them even by 'the Rothschilds.' These last, of course, are great caravanserais, with 'magnificent ladies' drawing-rooms' and 'replete' (a word that seems to have taken service with the licensed victuallers) 'with every luxury.' They make up (a term unfortunately suggestive of transformation) hundreds of beds; they have equipages and 'night chamberlains;' '*On y parle français*;' '*Man spricht Deutsch*.' Of some of these there is quite a little biography, beginning with the year of their establishment and narrating their happy union with other agreeable premises, like a brick and mortar novel. I remember them well: their 'romantic surroundings' or 'their exclusive privilege of meeting trains upon the platform;' their accurate resemblance to 'a gentleman's own house' (with 'a reception-room 80 feet by 90 feet'); their 'douche and spray baths;' their 'unexceptionable tariff;' and even their having undergone those 'extensive alterations,' through which I also underwent something, which they did not allow for in the bill.

These hotels are all more or less satisfactory as to appearance; furnished, not, indeed, with such taste, nor so lavishly, as their rivals on the Continent, but handsomely enough; they are much cleaner than foreign inns; and if their reference to 'every sanitary improvement which science can suggest' is a little tall, even for an advertisement, one never has cause to shudder as happens in some places in France proper and in Brittany everywhere. Though it must be admitted that *tables d'hôte* abroad are not the banquets which the travelling Briton believes them to be, our own hotel public dinners are inferior to their originals, and, what is very hard, those who pay for an entertainment in private suffer from them. The guest who happens to dine later than the *table d'hôte* in his own apartment can hardly escape getting things 'warmed up;' and if he dines at the same time he has nobody to wait on him. There is one thing that presses with great severity on paterfamilias—the charge which is made at many of the large hotels of 1s. 6d. a day for attendance on each person. Half a guinea a week for service is a high price even for a bachelor; but when this has to be paid for every member of the family, it is ruinous. Young ladies who dine at the same table and do not give half the trouble of 'single gentlemen' ought not to be taxed in this way. It is urged by many that since attendance is charged in the bill,' there should be no other fees. But the lover of comfort will always cheerfully pay for a little extra civility; nor do I think that this practice—any more than that of feeing our railway porters—is a public disadvantage. The waiter does not know till the guest goes whether he is a person of inflexible principles or not, and, therefore, hope ameliorates his manners and shapes his actions to all. As to getting 'attendance' out of the bill, now it has once got into it, that I believe to be impossible. There it is, like the moth in one's drawing-room sofa. And yet I am old enough to remember how poor Albert Smith plumed himself on the benefit he bestowed upon the public, as he had imagined, by introducing a fixed charge for all services and doing away with 'Please, sir, boots.' In this country, and, to say truth, in most others, 'Please, sir, boots,' is indigenous and not to be done away with. We did very much better under the voluntary system, although a few people who did not deserve it, but simply could not afford to be lavish, were called in consequence 'screws.'

To pay the wages of another man's servants is absurd, and reminds one of the 'plate, glass, and linen' that used to be charged for at the posting-house on the Dover road with every threepenny-worth of brandy-and-water, I have been asked 6d. for an orange (when oranges were cheap) at a London hotel, upon the ground that they never charged less than 6d. for anything; and I have read of 'an old established and family hotel' near Piccadilly, where the charge for putting the *Times* upon a guest's breakfast-table was 6d. up to this present year of grace. 'Gentlemen and families had always been supplied with it at that price,' said the landlord, when remonstrated with, 'and it was his principle, and his customers approved it, to keep things as they were.' It must be admitted, however, that matters have changed for the better in this respect elsewhere; and, at all events, the printed tariff that may now be consulted in every modern hotel enables you to know what you are spending.

Things are improved, too, in the way of light and air; both the public and private rooms of our hotels are far more cheerful and better appointed than they used to be, and instead of the four-posters there are French beds. The one great advantage that our new system possesses over the old is, indeed, the sleeping accommodation. The 'skimpy' mattress, the sheet that used to come untucked through shortness, leaving the feet tickled by the blanket, and the thin, limp thing that called itself a feather bed, are only to be found in ancient hostelries.

On the other hand, it must be confessed that the food has deteriorated; the bill of fare, indeed, is more pretentious, but the materials are inferior, and so is the cooking. The well-browned fowl, with its rich gravy and the bread-sauce that used to be its homely but agreeable attendant, has disappeared. The bird appears now under a French title, and is in other respects unrecognisable; as an Irish gentleman once explained it to me, it is not only that the thing appears under an *alias*, but the *alias* comes up instead of the thing. There is one essential which the old hotel often omitted to serve with your chicken, and which the new hotel supplies—the salad. This, however, few hotel cooks in England—and far less hotel waiters—can be trusted to prepare. Their simple plan is to deluge the tender lettuce with some hateful ingredient called 'salad mixture,' poured out of a peculiarly shaped bottle, such as the law now compels poisons to be sold in; and the jewel is deserving of its casket—it is almost poison. Nor, alas! is security always to be attained by making one's salad for one's self. For supposing even that the lettuce is fresh and white, and not manifestly a cabbage that is pretending to be a lettuce, how about the oil? Charles Dickens used to say that he could always tell the character of an inn from its cruets; if they were dirty and neglected, all was bad. The cruets are now clean enough in all hotels of pretension; but alas for that bottle which should contain (and perhaps did at some remote period contain) the oil of Lucca! On the fingers of one hand I could count all the hotels in

England which have not given me bad oil. Whether it was never good, or whether it has gone bad, I leave to those philosophers who investigate the origin of evil. I only know that it tastes as hair-oil smells. As to the soups, they are no worse than they used to be, and no better; there is soup and there is hotel soup.

'Gravy soup, fried sole, *entrée*, leg of mutton, and apple tart' used to be the unambitious *menu* of the old-fashioned inn. The *entrée* was terrible, but the fish, meat, and sweet were excellent. I will say nothing of the *entrées* now; I am not in a position to say anything, for not being of a sanguine temperament, and having but a few years to live, I do not venture upon them. But it is undeniable that our bill of fare is greatly more varied than it used to be, and that the way in which the table is arranged is much more attractive. At the great hotels in the neighbourhood of London where rich, or at all events prodigal people, go to dine in the summer months, this is especially the case. All these establishments affect fine dinners, yet how seldom it is they give you good ones! Their wines, though monstrously dear, are very fair; indeed, of the champagnes at least you may make certain by looking at the corks; but the food! How many of their fancifully named dishes might be included under the common title, Fiasco!

It was once suggested to a decayed man of fashion that an excellent profession for him to take up would be the proprietorship of an hotel of this class. 'You know what is really worth eating,' said an influential friend of his, 'and these caterers for your own class evidently don't; if you will undertake the management of the *Mammoth* (naming an inn of very high repute), I will furnish the funds.' But the man of fashion, who had spent his all with very little to show for it, had at least acquired some knowledge of his fellow-creatures. 'I am deeply obliged to you,' he said, 'but were I to accept your offer I should only lose your money. There are but a very few people in the world who know a good dinner when it is set before them; and a very large class (including all the ladies, who are only solicitous about its *looking* good) do not care whether it is good or bad. In private life if a dinner consists of many courses, is given at a fine house, and is presumably expensive, nineteen-twentieths of those who sit down to it are satisfied. The twentieth alone says to himself, 'How much better I should have dined at home!' I have been at scores and scores of great dinner-parties where the very plates were cold and nobody but myself has observed it.'

I have no doubt the gentleman of fashion was right; delicate cooking would be entirely thrown away upon the general palate. The fair sex, the young, the hungry, the easy-going, the ignorant—how large a majority of the 'frequenters' of hotels do these classes embrace! And it must also be remarked that to cook food (except whitebait) delicately in large quantities is a very difficult operation indeed.

Upon the whole, I think, our large hotels, 'arranged on the Continental system,' are well adapted for those who frequent them, and they show a readiness to adopt improvements. An immense number of well-to-do people go to Brighton, to Scarborough, and scores of other places to get a change and fresh air, but also to find the same amusements to which they have been accustomed in London; and, on the whole, they get what they want without paying very much too much for it. But what drives many quiet folks abroad is their disinclination to meet with all this gaiety and public life; they do not mind it so much when it is mixed with the foreign element, and they are also under the impression that picturesque scenery is a peculiarity of the Continent. I believe that more English people have visited Switzerland than have seen the Lake District and the Channel Islands, and very many more than have travelled in North Devon and Cornwall. The chief reason of their abstinence in this respect is, however, their dread of the want of 'accommodation.' To the last two counties, with the exception of some towns, such as Ilfracombe, approachable by sea, or a direct railway route, folks never go in crowds, and never will go. It is true there are no mammoth hotels to be found there; but for picturesque situation and a certain homely comfort, that takes one not only into another world, but another generation, there is nothing equal to certain little inns in these out-of-the-way places. In Wales also, and even in the Isle of Wight, there are perfect bowers of bliss of this description, still undesecrated by the excursionist. Not ten years ago, in a part of North Devon which shall be nameless, I came, with my wife and daughter, upon an inn of this description. We were all enraptured with the exquisite beauty of its situation, and were so imprudent as to express, in the presence of the landlady, our wish to live and die there. 'Well, indeed, sir,' she said, 'I am delighted to see you, but I hope you are not going to stay very long.' 'My dear madam,' I remonstrated, aghast at this remark, 'are we, then, such very objectionable-looking persons?' 'Bless your heart, no, sir, it isn't that; but the fact is, we have only room for three, and if parties come and come, and always find us full (through your being here, you know), they will think it is no use coming, and we shall lose our custom.' We did stay on, however, a pretty long time—it was a place of ineffable beauty, such as one parts from almost with tears—and when on our departure I asked for my bill, the landlady said, 'Dear me, sir, would you kindly tell me what day you come upon, for I ha' lost my account of it?' The life we led at that inn was purely pastoral; the clotted cream was of that consistency that it was meat and drink in one; but although the fare was homely, it was good of its kind, and admirably cooked. There was fresh fish every day—for we were too far from railways for that Gargantuan ogre, 'the London market,' to deprive us of it—and tender fowls, and jams of all kinds such as no money could buy.

The landlady had a genius for making what she called 'conserves,' and every cupboard in the queer little house was filled with them. In the sitting-room was a quantity of old china and knick-knacks, brought by the sailors of the place from foreign lands; the linen was white as snow, and smelt of lavender. Outside the inn was a sea that stretched to Newfoundland, and cliffs that caught the sunset—such scenery as is not surpassed by that of the Tyrol (though, of course, in a very different line), and be sure I was afraid of no comparison between our 'Travellers' Rest' and any Tyrolean inn. It is noteworthy that this hostelry of ours was so peculiarly and picturesquely placed that it could only be approached on foot, which reminds me of another place of entertainment for man, but not for beast.

In appearance, 'The Strangers' Welcome' (as I will take leave to term it) is more ambitious than 'The Rest,' but it is of the same simple type. In some respects it is even more primitive; no sign hangs over its door, nor is any other symbol of its vocation visible, 'Liberty,' not 'License,' as one may say without much metaphor, being its motto. It is on an island, so insignificant in extent that horse exercise is impossible on it. What it lacks in superficial area is more than made up, however, in its stupendous height. From the 'Welcome,' though it lies in a dell, one looks down perhaps a hundred sheer feet upon the ocean. Its solemn murmur, even in calm, always reaches the place, and when in storm, its spray. As one watches it from the lawn among the fuchsias, one scarcely knows which mood becomes it best. The fuchsias grow against our walls and tap at our window-panes in the morning as though they were roses; they even make their homes in the rocks, like the conies. The island is a very garden of fuchsias, tall as trees; and there are no other trees. The 'Welcome' itself is a sort of farmhouse without the farm; there is a goat or two and a donkey to be seen about it, which would account for the milk having an alien flavour, if it had one. But the 'Welcome' has excellent milk, so that there must be some cows somewhere. From the cliff-top you may see Alderney, for our inn is among the Channel Islands. When a storm comes you must stop where you are; for until the last waves of it have ceased there is no approach to us from the world without. To the stranger it seems probable at such seasons that the little place will burst up from below, for beneath it are caverns innumerable, filled with furious waves like sea monsters roaring for our lives. The sea, in short, has honeycombed it, and renews her vows to be its ruin with every gale. Yet the 'Welcome' lasts our time, and will last that of many generations, who will continue, however, doubtless to believe that the sublimities of Nature are unattainable short of Switzerland.

My memory now transports me to a mountain district in the north, but on this side of the border; and here, again, the inn is signless, and has no appearance of an inn at all. It is situated on the last of a great chain of hills, with lakes among them. It has lawns and shrubberies, but few flowers; Nature frowns on every hand, even in sunshine, when the waterfalls flow like silver, and the crags are decked with diamonds. There are no 'trencher-scraping, napkin-carrying,' waiters in the house, but country damsels attend upon you, and a motherly dame, their mistress, expresses her hope every morning that you have slept well. If you have not, it is the fault of your conscience: you have had a poet's recipe for it, for you have been 'within the hearing of a hundred streams' all night. Will you go up the Fells, or will you row on the Lake? These are your simple alternatives; there is no brass band, no promenade, no pier, no anything that the vulgar like. Yet once a week at least a great spectacle can be promised you without crossing the inn threshold (indeed, when the promise is kept it is better to be on the right side of it)—a thunder-storm among the hills. The arrangements for lighting the place, of which you may have complained, not without reason, are then in perfection, and the silence is broken with a vengeance. It is difficult to imagine the grandeurs of a sham-fight—a battle without corpses—but here you have them. First the musketry, then the guns, with the explosion of the powder-magazine—repeated about forty times by the mountain echoes—at the end of it. When all is over you sit down to such a supper as Lucullus would have given a year of life for, and which, in all probability—for he had no prudence—would have shortened it for him. At the 'Retreat,' as it is called, among other native delicacies, they give you fresh char cooked to a turn. I like to think that this was the fish that Monte Christo had sent him in a tank to Paris on the occasion of a certain banquet; but all the wealth of the Indies could not have accomplished that; the char (in spite of its name) does not travel.

One more reminiscence of country inns; and, though I have more of them in the picture-gallery of my memory, I have done. I conjure up an ivy-covered dwelling, long roofed but low, and sheltered by a lofty hill. Its situation is quite solitary, and, save for the cry of the seagull, there reigns about it an unbroken silence. It is on the very highway of the world, but the road is noiseless, for it is the sea. From the windows, all day long, we can watch the ships pass by that carry the pilgrims of the earth, for their freight is chiefly human. It is here 'the first ray glitters on the sail that brings our friends up from the under world, and the last falls on that which sinks with all we love below the verge.' Even at night there is no cessation to this coming and going; only, a red light or a white, and the distant strokes of a paddle-wheel in the hush of the moonless void are then the sole signs of all this motion. What hopes and fears contend in unseen hearts under those moving stars! Is it nothing to have the opportunity to watch them from the ivied porch of the 'Outlook,' and to welcome the thoughts they arouse within us? On land, too, there are stars, not made in heaven, but their shining is intermittent. As I lie in my bed I can see the great revolving light on the farthest point of rock that juts to sea. That is the 'Outlook's' watchman, not of much use to it, indeed, in a practical way, but imparting a marvellous sense of guardianship and security.

The chief means of amusement at inns of this kind is supplied by science in the telescope. You note through it all that comes and goes, and after a day or two can tell-for yourself whither each stately ship is bound, or whence it comes. At the 'Outlook' the food is plain, but good; the prawns in particular (which the young people, by-the-bye, can catch for themselves) are of an exquisite flavour, and in size approach the lobster. Twice a week for four hours this earthly Paradise is as a town taken by assault and given over to pillage. An excursion steamer stops at the little pier and discharges a cargo of excursionists. But those to whom the happiness of their fellow-creatures is intolerable can withdraw themselves at these seasons to the neighbouring Downs and Bays, and on their return they will find peace with folded wing sitting as before on the 'Outlook's' flagstaff.

Such are the inns which I have known, and there are hundreds in beautiful England like them. On its rivers in particular there are many charming little inns, but, to say truth, although the gentlemen-fishermen are as quiet as mice (from their habits of caution in their calling), the disciples of the oar are noisy; they get up too early and go to bed too late, and are too much addicted to melody. Moreover, these houses of entertainment often carry the principle of home production to excess: their native fare is excellent; but, spring mattresses not growing in the neighbourhood, the stuffing of the beds is supplied, to judge by results, from the turnip-field. For the purpose for which they are intended, however, these little hostels are well fitted and have a river charm that is indescribable.

I could speak, too, of excellent hotels set in the grounds of ruined castles or abbeys; but the attractions of the latter interfere with the repose of the visitor. Moreover, it has been my chief object, while admitting the merits of the *Crown* (and) *Imperial*, to paint the lily—to point out the violet half hid from the eye. It seems to me a pity that so many persons should leave their native land and spend their money among foreigners through ignorance of the quiet resting-places that await them at home. I have in no way exaggerated their merits, but it must be confessed that they have one serious drawback, which, however, only affects bachelors; if Paterfamilias is troubled by it he ought to be ashamed of himself. I allude to the happy couples on their honeymoon whom one is wont to meet with in these retired bowers. It is aggravating, no doubt, to see how Angelina and Edwin devote themselves to one another without the slightest regard for the feelings of the solitary stranger. The poor creature has no wish, of course, to thrust his company upon them, still he would like to have his existence acknowledged; and they ignore it. They have not a word to throw to him, nor even a glance. Then there are certain endearments, delightful, no doubt, to those who exchange them, but which to the spectator are distraction. What I would recommend to the bachelor as a remedy is a wife of his own. The good Mussulman's idea of future happiness is a perpetual honeymoon; and these little Paradises are the very places to spend it in. The customs of our own country forbid the agreeable variety which has such charms for the Faithful; but, even as it is, I have seen in these pleasant inns a great deal of human happiness, such as to the sober lover of his species only adds to their attraction.

MAID-SERVANTS.

It is a common thing to hear the remark expressed by much-tried mistresses that servants are not 'reasonable beings.' The observation may either have been provoked by the misbehaviour of some particular domestic, or by the injudicious defence of the class by one of the male sex. For the gentlemen have more to urge in favour of our domestics than the ladies have, and, as the latter maintain, for a very obvious reason—'they have much less to do with them.' The statement is cynical, but correct. So long as a man finds his clothes brushed and his meals well and punctually cooked, he 'does not see much to complain of,' nor does he give much thought to the pains and trouble which even that moderate amount of service entails upon his wife. Unless in great households, where everything is delegated to a paid housekeeper, it is, indeed, certain that ladies who are resolved to keep a house as it should be have, now, from various causes, a very hard time of it. The old feeling of feudal service, though a few examples—both mistresses and servants—may still exist of it, is dead; and in its place we have the employer and the hireling. There are faults, of course, on both sides; mistresses are accustomed to look upon their servants too much as machines, and in the working thereof do not, perhaps, estimate sufficiently the advantages of the use of sweet oil; while servants are more prone to 'eye-service' than were ever the housemaids of Ephesus. Which of the two began it I cannot tell, but a certain antagonism has grown up between these two classes which shakes the pillars of domestic peace. At the root of it all, as at the root of most evils, lies ignorance, and in the servants' case ignorance of a stupendous nature.

I have had in my household an under-nurse, who, upon the family's leaving town for a short holiday, was enjoined to see that the birds in the nursery (canaries) were well supplied with sand. When we came back we found them all starved to death. She had given them sand, but, alas! no seed. This was a girl from the country, who, one would think, would have known what birds fed upon; otherwise one does not expect much intelligence from Arcadia. When our last importation (an under-housemaid) 'turned on the gas' in the upper apartments as she was directed to do, but omitted to light it, I thought it very excusable; she had not been accustomed to gas. On the other hand, when her mistress told her to 'look to the fire' of a certain room, I contend we had a right to expect that that fire should be kept in. It was not so, however, and when the lady inquired, 'Why did you not look to it, as I told you?' the girl replied, 'Well, I did, mum; the door was open and I looked at the fire every time I passed.' She appeared to attach some sort of igneous power to the human eye.

Each of these young ladies came to us very highly recommended by the wife of the clergyman of her native place. Surely, in the curriculum of the village school, something else beside the catechism ought to have been included; yet, of the things they were certain to be set to do—the merest first principles of domestic service—they had been taught nothing; and in learning them at our expense they cost us ten times their wages.

It may be said, indeed, that when you employ a young girl who has never been out to service before, you secure honesty, chastity, and sobriety, and must not look for the artificial virtues; but, unhappily, things are not very much better when you engage an experienced hand. The lady of the house should not, of course, expect too much (in these days she must be of a very sanguine temperament if she falls into *that* error); she will think it necessary to warn the new arrival—although she 'knows her place' and is 'a thorough housemaid'—that a velvet pile carpet, for example, should not be brushed backwards. But on more obvious matters she will probably leave the 'thorough housemaid' to her own devices, the result of which is that the boards beside the stair-carpets are washed with soda the first morning, which takes the dirt off effectually—and the paint also. An hour or two before she was caught at this, she has, perhaps, utterly spoilt a polished grate or two by rubbing them with scouring paper instead of emery powder.

Paterfamilias feels these things when he has to pay the bill, but his wife feels them in the meantime, and it is more than is to be expected of human nature that she can welcome cordially such an addition to her household. A prejudice against the girl springs up in her mind, which is very promptly responded to, and the mutual respect that ought to grow up between them is nipped in the bud. I am sorry to say that good housewives are almost always opposed to having servants well educated; they think that 'knowledge puffs up,' blows them above their places, and encourages a taste for light literature which is opposed to the arts of brushing and cleaning. What the 'higher education' of domestic servants is to be under the School Boards I know not; but I hope they will not imagine, as the Universities do, that their duty is only to teach their pupils how to educate themselves. I confess I agree with the housewives, that, for young persons intended for service, reading, writing, and arithmetic, with the use of the scrubbing and hearth brushes, are far preferable acquirements to those of the same three great principles with the use of the globes. Whether there are any handbooks in existence, other than cookery books, to teach the duties of servants I know not; but, even if there are, servants will never read them of their own free will. Not one in a hundred has a sufficiently strong desire to improve herself for that. They must be taught like children, and when they *are* children, if any good is to come of it.

It is to me astounding, and certainly makes me very suspicious of the advocates of women's rights, that they have done little or nothing in this direction. Why should not some of that immense energy which is now expended on platforms be directed into this less ambitious but more natural channel? There are tens of thousands of persons of their own sex, not indeed out of employment, but who are obtaining employment on false pretences, who would do so honestly enough if they had had but a little early training. Unfortunately, the ladies of the platform do not in general stoop to such small things as domestic matters; they do not care about mere comfort, they even perhaps resent it because it is so dear to tyrannous man. If they would only turn their attention to the education of their humbler sisters, they would win over all their enemies and put to shame the cynic who has associated Man's Lefts with Women's Rights.

The only School for Servants I am acquainted with sent us the worst we ever had, and if it had not been for the very handsome fee it charged both us and her for our mutual introduction, I should not have recognised it as an educational establishment at all.

It will naturally be said by men (not by their wives, for they know better), 'But surely self-interest will cause a servant to qualify herself for a place, since, having done so, she will command better wages.' This is the mistake of the political economists, who, right enough in the importance they attach to self-interest, gravely err in supposing it to be always of a material kind. They start with the idea that everybody wants to make as much money as possible. So they do; but with a large majority this desire is subordinate to the wish for leisure and enjoyment. Trades unionism, with all its faults, is founded on this important fact in human nature—that many of us prefer narrow means, with comparative leisure, to affluence with toil. That this notion, if universal, would destroy good work of all kinds and make perfection impossible, is beside the question, or certainly never enters into the minds of those chiefly concerned in the matter. 'A good day's work for a good day's wage' is a fine sentiment; but 'half a day's work for half a day's wage' suits some people even better; while 'half a day's work for a good day's wage' suits them better still. In old times the sense of 'service being no inheritance' begat habits of good conduct as well as thrift, for in most well-conducted households, servants' wages were made proportionate to their length of service. But nowadays a lady's promise of raising a servant's wages every year is quite superfluous, since it is ten to one against her keeping her for the first twelve months. It is no wonder, then, that while the conviction of service being of a temporary character is, at least, as strong as ever, the course of conduct it now suggests is to make as much as possible out of it while it lasts, in the way of perquisites, etc. With our cooks, especially, it is not too much to say that wages are often a secondary object as compared with the opportunity of making a purse for themselves; and the recognised privilege of selling the dripping affords cover for a multitude of petty delinquencies which if not positive thefts have a strong family resemblance to them.

Before leaving the subject of short terms of service, it should be noted that the modern servant openly avows her love of change. An excellent mistress, and a very kind one, has told me that housemaids and kitchenmaids have given her warning again and again for no other cause than this. They have avowed themselves quite happy and contented in their place, but they want 'fresh woods and pastures new.' When Jack Mytton was reminded by his lawyer that a certain estate he was about to sell had been in his family for 500 years, he replied, 'Then it's high time it should go out of it;' and the same reflection occurs to our Janes and Bessies. They have been in their present situation a year perhaps, or two at most—indeed, two years is considered in the world below stairs the extreme point for any person of spirit to remain under one roof—and it is high time they should leave it. One would naturally think that, in the case of young women at all events, they would be slow to exchange even a moderately comfortable place for a home among strangers; that they would bear the ills they know of, even if ills exist, rather than venture on those of which they know nothing; but this is far from being the case. Nor do they even quit their place in order 'to better themselves.' They have absolutely no reason except the love of change. Behaviour of this sort naturally gives some colour to the remark already quoted that servants are not 'reasonable beings.' I was almost a convert to that opinion myself when, on one occasion, having asked a female domestic to be good enough to put my boots on the tree, she literally obeyed my order. She hung all my boots on the tree in the garden, and it was very wet weather. But to young persons who come from the country everything is pardonable—except 'temper.'

The growth of this parasite in both town and country is, however, quite alarming. Little as mistresses dare to say to the disadvantage of servants when leaving their employment, no matter for what reason, they do sometimes remark of them that their temper is 'uncertain.' When this happens and the fact is communicated to Jane or Betsy by the lady to whom they have proposed themselves, they have one invariable method of self-defence: 'Temper, mum? Well, I 'ave my faults, I daresay, but not *that*; all as knows me knows my temper is 'eavenly. But the fact is, mum, Mrs. Jones [her late mistress] was a bit flighty.' And she touches her forehead, and even sometimes winks, to indicate aberration of the intellect. A really good-tempered servant is now rare; and there are very few who will bear 'speaking to' when their work is neglected or ill-done.

What, however, always puts them in the highest good humour is an expensive breakage. When Susan comes to say, 'Oh, please, mum, I've 'ad a haccident with the pier glass,' her face is wreathed in smiles. To a mistress who cannot relieve her feelings by strong language, as a man would do, this behaviour is very aggravating. If servants do not actually delight in these misfortunes, I am afraid not one in twenty shows the least consideration for her employer's purse. It is charitable to say, when Thomas or Jane leaves the gas burning all night, or the sun-blinds out in the pouring rain, that they have 'no head;' but it is my experience that they are very careful, and, indeed, take quite extraordinary precautions, with respect to their own property. I am afraid that the true reason of the waste and extravagance among servants is that they have no attachment to their employers, and of course it is less troublesome to be lavish than to be economical. All the education in the world cannot make selfish persons unselfish; but it can surely implant in them some sense of duty. At present, so long as a servant is not absolutely dishonest, her conscience rarely troubles her. This is especially the case with our cooks, who also—that 'dripping' question making their path so slippery—draw the line between honesty and its contrary very fine indeed.

Moreover, they know less of what they pretend to know than any other class of servant. The proof of this is in the fact that not one in a hundred of them will cook you a dinner on trial. I have often said to a cook, 'Your character is satisfactory enough in other respects; but, before engaging you, will you show what you can do by sending up one good dinner, for which I will pay you at the ordinary rate —namely, half-a-guinea?' She won't do it; she says she can cook for a prince, and affects to be hurt at the proposition. The consequence is that for a month, at least, we are slowly poisoned. Once only I hired a cook who accepted these terms. I am bound to say she sent us up a most excellent dinner, but when I sent for her to pay the half-guinea she was dead drunk on the kitchen floor. She had taken a bottle of port wine and one of stout while serving up that entertainment, and afterwards confessed that during her arduous duties she required 'constant support.' Again, it is by no means unusual for cooks to succeed to admiration for a week and then to begin to spoil everything, the proverb respecting a 'new broom' applying, curiously enough, even more to them than to the 'housemaids.'

These observations are no doubt severe, but they are not unjust; nor do I for a moment imply that servants are always to blame, and never mistresses. There are faults on both sides. Ladies often show themselves as 'unreasonable' as their female domestics. For example, although very solicitous for the settlement of their own daughters in life, they often do not give sufficient opportunities for their maid-servants to find husbands. A girl in service is quite as anxious to get a husband as her young mistresses, and, indeed, it is of much more consequence for her to do so. She sees her youth slipping away from her in a place where no 'followers' are allowed, and it is no wonder that she 'wants a change.' She has a right to have her holidays and her 'Sundays out,' and it is the mistress's duty not only to grant them, but to make some inquiry as to how she spends them. Many ladies who go to church with much regularity never take the smallest interest in the moral conduct of those to whom they stand, morally if not legally, *in loco parentis*, and who may, perhaps, have no other adviser.

Mistresses of all ranks, too, show a lamentable want of principle in the matter of character-giving. It wants, no doubt, a certain strength of mind to write the truth. 'The girl is going, thank Heaven,' they say to themselves, and they are glad to get rid of her, without a row, at the easy price of a small falsehood. They lay the flattering unction to their souls that they are concealing certain facts in order 'not to stand in the way of the poor girl's future.' What they are really doing is an act of selfishness, cruel as regards the lady who is trusting to their word, and baneful as regards the public good. It is the good characters which make the bad servants. In a certain primitive district of England, where ministers are 'called' from parish to parish, one of the churchwardens of X complained to the churchwardens of Y that his late importation from the Y pulpit was not very satisfactory. 'And yet,' he said, 'you all cracked him up enormously.' 'Yes,' replied the churchwarden of Y, 'and you will have to crack him up too before you get rid of him.'

Now, it is only ignorance which causes ladies to believe that there is any necessity to 'crack up' the character of a servant. They are not obliged (though, of course, if the servant has behaved well it would be infamous to withhold it) to give her any character at all, and they may state the most unpleasant truth (if they are quite certain of the fact and can prove it) without the least fear of an action for libel. The law does not punish them for telling the truth about their servants, and in another matter also it is more just than it is supposed to be. There is a superstition among servants that when leaving their situations before their time is out they have a right to claim board wages, and that even when dismissed for gross misconduct they have a right to their ordinary wages for the remainder of the month; but these are mere popular errors. The only case with which I am acquainted where neither of these dues was demanded was rather a curious one. A widow lady advertised for a cook and a housemaid, and procured them by the first cast of her net. They came together with an open avowal of their previous acquaintanceship; they were attached to one another, they said, and did not wish to be in separate service, and wages were not so much an object to them as opportunities of friendship. The lady, who had an element of romance in her, was touched with this expression of sentiment; it was also a great convenience to her to be so quickly suited; and, their characters being good, she engaged them. They had come from a house of much greater pretensions than her own, and had taken higher wages, which might have attracted her suspicions; but she had very little work for them to do, and she concluded that 'an easy place' had had its attractions for them. Her servants were well treated and well fed, and were allowed to see their friends; but she objected to evening visits, and required the back door to be locked and the key placed in her possession at nine o'clock every evening. If the front door was opened she could hear it from every part of her modest residence (and, being very nervous, she used often to fancy that it opened when it did not), while a wire for the use of the policeman connected the ground-floor with an alarm bell in her own room in case of fire or other contingency. The two servants had been six days with her when this alarm bell was pealed one night with great violence. She looked out of window, and beheld a cab laden with luggage standing at her door. She expected nobody; but whoever had come was more welcome than 'thieves' or 'fire,' and she went up to the maid's room to bid them answer the door. She found to her great astonishment—for it was two in the morning—the apartment empty, and while she was there the alarm-bell sounded again with increased fury. Looking over the balusters, she perceived a light in the hall and inquired who was there. 'Well, it's us two,' returned the cook, 'we're just agoin, so good-bye. It ain't at all the sort o' place for us, and you ain't the sort o' missis.' Then there was a shout of laughter, the front door was opened and slammed to, and the cab drove off with its tenants, leaving their mistress to her lonely meditations. The two friends had come on trial, it seemed, and had had enough of it.

That they made no claim for wages of any kind seems quite curious when one considers what sort of servants, and in what sort of circumstances, do demand them. And, as a rule, masters and mistresses give in to the extortion. Yet the law is on their side, nor have they any reason to complain of it in other respects. The improvement that is needed is in themselves, and in their relations to those in their employment. Our young ladies are so engaged in their accomplishments and their amusements that they have no time to acquire a knowledge of domestic affairs, so that when they marry they know no more of a housewife's duties than their husbands. No wonder men of moderate means shrink from marriage when wives have become a source of discomfort and expense, instead of their contraries, and have lost the name of helpmate. How can they be in a position to teach their servants when they themselves are grossly ignorant of what they would have them learn? There are certain village schools, indeed, which profess to train their pupils for domestic service, but they only teach them to be maids-of-all-work, the least remunerated and the hardest-worked of all the daughters of toil. They offer no premium to diligence and perfection.

This state of things is very hard both upon mistresses and servants, but it is not irremediable, and the remedy must come from the upper of the two classes. Schools are as necessary for servants as they are for other people; they must be taught their calling before they can practise it; and schools for servants must therefore be instituted. With schools will come certificates of merit, and servants will then be paid for what they can really do, and not, as now, in proportion to their powers of audacity of assertion.

MEN-SERVANTS.

The subject of men-servants is by no means of such universal interest as that of maid-servants, and those who suffer from them are not only less numerous, but less deserving of pity; as a lady of limited means once put it in my hearing, 'They can better afford to be robbed and murdered' On the other hand, whatever truth may be in the dogma that where a woman is bad she is worse than a bad man, it is certain that when a man-servant is bad he can do more mischief than a bad maid-servant. In many cases he is a necessity, not because folks are rich, but because they have large families, and the service is consequently too heavy to be undertaken solely by women. I have known many householders who, weary of the trouble and annoyance given by men-servants, have resolved to engage only those of the other sex, and who have had to resort to men-servants again for what may be called physical reasons.

When this happens, however, both master and mistress should agree to the arrangement, or at all events be both informed that it has been made. Only last autumn a lady friend of mine adopted it in the absence of her husband abroad, and forgot to apprise him of it by letter. He arrived home late at night, and, letting himself in with a latch-key, took the strange man for a burglar, and was almost the death of him by strangulation before he could explain that he was the new butler.

No woman can bring up a luncheon or dinner tray for a dozen people twice a day without sooner or later coming to grief with it. And here it is appropriate to say that in places where there is much heavy work it is only reasonable that wages should be higher than where the work is light. Whereas, upon such irrational grounds is our whole system of domestic service built, that this is hardly ever taken into consideration. Since the servant is told beforehand what he or she will have to do, it is taken for granted that the conditions are acceptable to them; whereas, the fact is that the capability of performing their duties is the very last thing to enter their minds. They cannot afford to remain 'out of a situation,' and therefore take the first that offers itself as a stopgap, with no more intention of permanently remaining there than a European who accepts an appointment in Turkey, and with the same object—namely, to make as much as possible out of the Turks in the meantime.

In the case of a man-servant, especially in London, no written character should ever be held sufficient. A personal interview with his late master or mistress is indispensable. This gives a little trouble, no doubt, on both sides; but those who grudge it, for such a purpose, must indeed be grossly selfish, and when they engage a ticket-of-leave man for their butler get no worse than they deserve. One of the best butlers, however, I ever knew was a ticket-of-leave man—engaged on the faith of a written character, which was, of course, a forged one, and who remained with his employer no less than eighteen months. If his speculations on the turf had been successful, he might have parted with him the best of friends, and perhaps have purchased a residence in the same square; but something went wrong with the brother to Bucephalus, whom he had backed for the Derby, and the poor man had to dispose of the whole of his master's family plate to pay his own debts of honour and defray his travelling expenses—probably to some considerable distance, as the police could never hear of him. The risk in taking a butler without a personal guarantee of at least his honesty and sobriety can indeed hardly be exaggerated. If a clever fellow, his influence over his fellow-servants of the other sex is very great, and it is a recognised maxim of the class never 'to tell upon one another' so long as they remain good friends. I have heard an experienced housewife say there is nothing she dreads so much as an unbroken harmony below stairs; like silence in the nursery, it is ominous of all sorts of mischief.

Of course, the ticket-of-leave man was an extreme case; but it is certain that some butlers who are not thieves are always treading on the very confines of roguery. They are like trustees who, though they will not touch the principal entrusted to them, not only omit to put it out to the best advantage, but will sometimes even pocket a portion of the interest 'for their trouble.' I remember reading a curious case of this sort. A gentleman who had been with his family in Switzerland for nine months was met by a London acquaintance on his return, who expressed his regret at his having been in trouble at home. 'Nay, I have been in no trouble,' he replied, 'and, indeed, none of us have been at home.' 'But a month ago when I was passing down your street I surely saw a funeral standing at your door?' Nor had his eyes deceived him. The butler in charge had let the house for a couple of months, and but for his singular ill-luck in one of his tenants happening to die during their temporary occupation of it, he would have pocketed the rent (*minus* the money requisite to keep the maids' mouths shut) and his master would have been none the wiser. It is said that it is only when we have lost a friend that we come to value him at his true worth; and it is certain that it is only when one's butler has left us and the tongues of his fellow-servants are loosened that we come to learn his demerits—the difference between his real character and his written one. If he is a rogue, his evil influence remains behind him, and, next to the maidservants, it is the page who suffers most from it. He becomes—poor little fellow!—almost by necessity an accessory to his delinquencies, plays pilot-fish to the other's shark, and himself grows up to swell the host of bad servants and that army of martyrs their masters and mistresses.

A common cause of a butler's ruin, and for which he is much to be pitied, is his having married unfortunately. I had once a good servant whom I was very loth to lose, but whose departure became necessary from his constantly being visited by a wife in advanced stages of intoxication. Housewives generally prefer a married man for their servant, for reasons that are not inscrutable. I do not wish to differ from such good authorities. But though I have no objection to my butler being married, I do object to maintain his wife, which, if he be on good terms with the cook, there is a strong probability of my having to do. As to his own eating, Heaven forbid that I should grudge it to him; but it is curious and utterly subversive of all medical dogma that both men-servants and maidservants, who take, of course, comparatively little exercise, should, nevertheless, contrive to eat more apiece for dinner than two average Alpine climbers. Four meals a day, and three of them meat meals, is their usual rate of sustenance, and the food must not only be frequent and plentiful, but very good. It is a gratifying proof of the rapid influence of civilisation that the daughter of a farm-labourer, accustomed at home to consider bacon a treat and beef a windfall, will, after a month's experience of her London place, decline to eat cold meat of any kind, reject salt butter as 'not fit for a Christian,' and become quite a *connoisseur* as to the strength of bitter ale. Indeed, two of our present female domestics are 'recommended' to drink claret because beer makes them bilious. I do not mind giving them claret, but I think it hard that under such circumstances I should have had a butler give me warning because the female domestics are 'not select enough.' My own impression is, though I scarcely like to mention it, because he was a married man, that he considered them too plain.

The reasons, or at all events the professed reasons, which servants give for leaving their situations are sometimes very curious. One man left a family of my acquaintance because he said he was interfered with by the young ladies. 'Good gracious, what do you mean?' inquired his mistress. Her daughters, it appears, were accustomed to arrange the flowers for the dinner-table, whereas, as he imagined, he had a peculiar gift for that kind of decoration himself.

On the other hand, it is sometimes difficult for a sensitive master or mistress to give the true reason for their parting with a servant. A friend of mine had a footman who, through trick, or some defect in his respiratory organs, used to blow like a grampus, and indeed more like a whale, while waiting at table. It was not a vice, of course, but it was very objectionable, and guests who were bald especially objected to it. My friend consulted with his butler, who admitted that 'John did blow like a pauper' (meaning, as I suppose, a porpoise), and undertook to break the subject to him. It is quite common to find candidates for service very deaf, and if they contrive to pass their 'entrance examination' (for which no doubt they sharpen their faculties), they stay with you for a month at least with an excellent excuse for making it a holiday, since, whatever you tell them to do they cannot hear and do not do it, or do something else which they like better. Mistresses who are silent about moral disqualifications are much more so, of course, about physical ones, and have no scruples in ridding themselves of a deaf man.

The worst class of men-servants, perhaps, are those who are said to 'require a master;' which means that when he happens to be not at home they neglect everything. A friend of mine who happened to take a week's holiday, alone, discovered on his return that his family might almost as well have had no servant at all as the man he left with them; he was generally out, and when at home had not even troubled himself to answer the drawing-room bell. Some men-servants are always running out; they have 'just stepped round the corner,' they say, 'to post a letter;' which in nine cases out of ten means to have a dram at the public-house. The servants who 'require a master' sometimes retain their situation with a very selfish one by devoting themselves to his service at the expense of the rest of the family. 'John suits me very well,' he says, 'and thoroughly understands his duties,' which in this case means the length of the master's foot.

On the other hand, there are some men-servants who, one would think, ought to belong to the other sex, so utterly ignorant they are of that branch of their duty which they call 'valeting.' A lady blessed with a scientific husband, who certainly did not take much notice whether he was 'valeted' or not, once complained to his man of his neglect in this particular. 'When your master comes in, William, you should look after him, and see to his hat and coat, and pay him little attentions.' So the next time the man of science came in he was not a little surprised by William (who, it is fair to say, came from the country) running up and taking his hat off his head, like some highly-trained retriever. Happy the master to whom a worse thing has never happened at the hands of his retainer!

The main thing to be dreaded in men-servants—next to downright dishonesty—is, of course, intoxication. If a man has been long in one's service and gets drunk for once and away, it may well be forgiven him; but when your new servant gets drunk, wait till he is sober enough to receive his wages, and then dismiss him—if you can. Not long ago I had occasion to discharge a butler for habitual intoxication; he was never quite drunk, but also never quite sober; he was a sot. I made him fetch a cab, and saw his luggage put upon it, and I tendered him his month's wages. But he refused to leave the house without board wages. Of course, I declined to pay him any such thing; and, as he persisted in leaning against the dining-room door murmuring at intervals, 'I wants my board wages,' I sent for a policeman. 'Be so good,' I said,' as to turn this drunken person out of my house.' 'I daren't do it, sir,' was the reply; 'that would be to exceed my duty.' 'Then, why are you here?' 'I am here, sir, to see that you turn the man out yourself without using unnecessary violence.' 'The man' was six feet high and as stout as a beer-barrel. I could no more have moved him than Skiddaw, and he knew it. 'I stays here,' he chanted in his maudlin way, 'till I gets my board wages.' Fortunately, two Oxford undergraduates happened to be in the house, to whom I mentioned my difficulty, and I shall not easily forget the delighted promptitude with which they seized upon the offender and 'ran him out' into the street. He fled down the area steps at once with a celerity that convinced me he was accustomed to being turned out of houses, and tried to obtain re-admission at the back-door. It was fortunately locked, but when I said to the policeman, '*Now*, please to remove that man,' he answered, 'No, sir; that would be to exceed my duty; he is still upon your premises and a member of your household.' As it was raining heavily, the delinquent, though sympathised with by a great crowd round the area railings, presently got tired of his position and went away. But supposing my young Oxford friends had not been in the house and he had fallen upon me (a little man) in the act of expulsion; or supposing I had been a widow lady with no protector, would that too faithful retainer have remained in my establishment for ever?

I have purposely addressed myself to that large class of the community only who are said 'to keep a man-servant'—that is, one man, assisted, perhaps, by a page. Those who keep butler, footman, coachman, grooms, and valets are comparatively few in number, and know nothing of the inconveniences which their less wealthy fellow-countrymen endure. In large establishments, if William is drunk, John is sober, and the work is done for the rich man by somebody; especially, too, if William is drunk, there are John and Thomas to turn him out of the house and have done with him. But it is certain that the lower Ten Thousand are not in a satisfactory condition as respects their men-servants; hardly more so, in fact, than the Hundred Thousand are in regard to their maids. The men-servants, however, are not so ignorant of their duties as are the latter, and if only their masters would have the courage to tell the truth when giving them their 'characters,' there would be a great improvement in them. Against the masters themselves (unlike the mistresses) I have never heard much complaint. Most of them object to be 'bothered' and 'troubled,' and are willing enough to put everything into their man's hands, including the key of the Cellar, if only they could trust him; but at present, alas! this is a very large 'If.'

WHIST-PLAYERS.

If cards are the Devil's books, Whist is the *édition de luxe* of them. Whist-playing is one of the few vices of the upper classes that has not in time descended to the lower, with whom the ingenious and attractive game of 'All Fours' has always held its own against it. I have known but two men not belonging to the upper ten thousand who played well at whist. One was a well-known jockey in the South of England, who was also, by the way, an admirable billiard-player. He called himself an amateur, but those who played with him used to complain that his proceedings were even ultra-professional. On the Turf men are almost as equal as they are under it, and this ornament of the pigskin would on certain occasions (race meetings) take his place at the card-table with some who were very literally his betters, while others who had more self-respect contented themselves with backing him. The other example I have in my mind was an ancient Cumberland yeoman, who, having lost the use of his limbs in middle life from having been tossed by a bull, pursued the science under considerable difficulties. A sort of card-rack (such as Psycho uses at the Egyptian Hall) was placed in front of him, and behind him stood his little granddaughter who played the cards for him by verbal direction. Both these men played a very good game of the old-fashioned kind, for though the jockey used subtleties, they were not of the Clay or Cavendish sort. The asking for trumps was a device unknown to him, though there were folks who whispered he would take them under certain circumstances without asking, and of the leading of the penultimate with five in the suit it could be said of him, for once, that he was as innocent as a babe.

Of course, many persons join the 'upper ten' who come from the lower twenty (or even thirty), and it need not be said that they are by no means inferior in sagacity to their new acquaintances; yet they rarely make first-rate players. Whist, like the classics, must be learnt young for any excellence to be attained in it. Of this Metternich was a striking example. If benevolent Nature ever intended a man for a whist-player one would have supposed that she had done so in his case, but had been baffled by some malign Destiny which had degraded him to that class by whom, in conjunction with Kings, it was fondly believed, previously to the recent general election, that 'the world was governed.' Until late in life he never took to whist, when he grew wildly fond of it, and played incessantly, till it is said a certain memorable event took place which caused him never to touch a card again. The story goes that, rapt in the enjoyment of the game, he suffered a special messenger to wait for hours, to whom if he had given his attention more promptly a massacre of many hundred persons would have been prevented. Humanity may drop a tear, but whist had nothing to regret in the circumstance; for in Metternich it did not lose a good player, and, what redeems his intelligence, he knew it. 'I learnt my whist too late,' he would say, with more pathos and solemnity, perhaps, than he would have used when speaking of more momentous matters of omission.

He must be a wise man indeed who, being an habitual whist-player, is aware that he is a bad one. In games of pure skill, such as chess, and, in a less degree, billiards, a man must be a fool who deceives himself upon such a point; but in whist there is a sufficient amount of chance to enable him to preserve his self-complacency for some time—let us say, his lifetime. If he loses, he ascribes it to his 'infernal luck,' which always fills his hands with twos and threes; and if he wins, though it is by a succession of four by honours as long as the string of four-in-hands when the Coaching Club meets in Hyde Park, he ascribes it to his skill. 'If I hadn't played trumps just when I did,' he modestly observes to his partner, 'all would have been over with us;' though the result would have been exactly the same had he played blindfold. To an observer of human nature, who is not himself a loser 'on the day,' there are few things more charming than the genial, gentle self-approval of two players of this class who have just defeated two experts, and proved, to their own satisfaction, that if fortune gives them 'a fair chance' or 'something like equal cards,' as they term the conditions of their late performance, they can play as well as other people.

Of course, the term 'good-play' is a relative one; the player who wins applause in the drawing-room is often thought but little of in places where the rigour of the game is observed; and the 'good, steady player' of the University Clubs is not a star of the first magnitude at the Portland. The best players used to be men of mature years; they are now the middle-aged, who, with sufficient practical experience, have derived their skill in early life from the best books. 'It is difficult to teach an old dog new tricks,' and for the most part the old dogs despise them. When I hear my partner boast that he is 'none of your book-players,' I smile courteously, and tremble. I know what will become of him and me if fortune does not give him his 'fair chance,' and I seek comfort from the calculation which tells me it is two to one against my cutting with him again. How marvellous it is, when one comes to consider the matter, that a man should decline to receive instruction on a technical subject from those who have eminently distinguished themselves in it, and have systematised for the benefit of others the results of the experience of a lifetime! With books or no books, it is quite true, however, that some men, otherwise of great intelligence, can never be taught whist; they may have had every opportunity of learning it—have been born, as it were, with the ace of spades in their mouth instead of a silver spoon—but the gift of understanding is denied them; and though it is ungallant to say so, I have never known a lady to play whist well.

In the case of the fair sex, however, it may be urged that they have not the same chances; they have no whist clubs, and the majority of them entertain the extraordinary delusion that it is wrong to play at whist in the afternoon. One may talk scandal over kettle-drums, and go to morning performances at the theatre, but one may not play at cards till after dinner. There is even quite a large set of male persons who, 'on principle,' do not play at whist in the afternoon. In seasons of great adversity, when fortune has not given me my 'fair chance' for many days, I have sometimes 'gone on strike,' as it is termed, and joined them; but anything more deplorable than such a state of affairs it is impossible to imagine. After their day's work is over, these good people can't conceive what to do with themselves, and, between ourselves, it is my experience, drawn from these occasional 'intervals of business,' that this practice of not playing whist in the afternoon generally leads to dissipation.

It is sometimes advanced by this unhappy class, by way of apology, that they play at night; which may very possibly be the case, but they don't play well. There is no such thing, except in the sense in which after-dinner speaking is called 'good,' as good whist after dinner. It may seem otherwise, even to the spectators; but having themselves dined like the rest, they are not in a position to give an opinion. The keenness of observation is blunted by food and wine; the delicate perceptions are gone; and what is left of the intelligence is generally devoted to finding faults in your partner's play. The consciousness of mistakes on your own part, which he is in no condition to discern, instead of suggesting charity, induces irritation, and you are persuaded, till you get the next man, that you are mated with the worst player in all Christendom. Moreover, that 'one more rubber' with which you propose to finish is generally elastic (*Indian* rubber), and you sit up into the small hours and find them disagree with you. If I ever write that new series of the 'Chesterfield Letters' which I have long had in my mind, and for which I feel myself eminently qualified, my most earnest advice to young gentlemen of fashion will be found in the golden rule, 'Never sit down to whist after dinner;' it is a mistake, and almost an immorality. If they must play cards, let them play Napoleon.

With regard to finding fault with one's partner, I have no apology to offer for it under any circumstances; but it must be remembered that this does not always arise from ill-temper, or the sense of loss that might have been gain. There are many lovers of whist for its own sake to whom bad play, even in an adversary, excites a certain distress of mind; when a good hand is thrown away by it, they experience the same sort of emotion that a gourmand feels who sees a haunch of venison spoilt in the carving. In such a case a gentle expression of disapproval is surely pardonable. And I have observed that, with one or two exceptions (*non Angli sed angeli*, men of angelic temper rather than ordinary Englishmen), the good players who never find fault are not socially the pleasantest. They are men who 'play to win,' and who think it very injudicious to educate a bad partner who will presently join the ranks of the Opposition.

What is rather curious—and I speak with some experience, for I have played with all classes, from the prince to the gentleman farmer—the best whist-players are not, as a rule, those who are the most highly educated or intellectual. Men of letters, for example (I am speaking, of course, very generally), are inferior to the doctors and the warriors. Both the late Lord Lytton and Charles Lever had, it is true, a considerable reputation at the whist-table, but though they were good players, they were not in the first class; while the author of 'Guy Livingstone,' though devoted to the game, was scarcely to be placed in the second. The best players are, one must confess, what irreverent persons, ignorant of the importance of this noble pursuit, would term 'idlers'—men of mere nominal occupation, or of none, to whom the game has been familiar from their youth, and who have had little else to do than to play it.

While some men, as I have said, can never be taught whist, a few are born with a genius for the game, and move up 'from high to higher,' through all the grades of excellence, with a miraculous rapidity; but, whether good, bad, or indifferent, I have not known half a dozen whist-players who were not superstitious. Their credulity is, indeed, proverbial, but no one who does not mix with them can conceive the extent of it; it reminds one of the African fetish. The country apothecary's wife who puts the ivory 'fish' on the candlestick 'for luck,' and her partner, the undertaker, who turns his chair in hopes to realise more 'silver threepences,' are in no way more ridiculous than the grave and reverend seigneurs of the Clubs who are attracted to 'the winning seats' or 'the winning cards.' The idea of going on because 'the run of luck' is in your favour, or of leaving off because it has declared itself against you, is logically of course unworthy of Cetywayo. The only modicum of reason that underlies it is the fact that the play of some men becomes demoralised by ill-fortune, and may, possibly, be improved by success. Yet the belief in this absurdity is universal, and bids fair to be eternal. 'If I am not in a draught, and my chair is comfortable, you may put me anywhere,' is a remark I have heard but once, and the effect of it on the company was much the same as if in the House of Convocation some reverend gentleman had announced his acceptance of the religious programme of M. Comte.

With the few exceptions I have mentioned, whist-players not only stop very far short of excellence in the game, but very soon reach their tether. I cannot say of any man that he has gone on improving for years; his mark is fixed, and he knows it—though he is exceptionally sagacious if he knows where it is drawn as respects others—and there he stays till he begins to deteriorate. The first warning of decadence is the loss of memory, after which it is a question of time (and good sense) when he shall withdraw from the ranks of the fighting men and become a mere spectator of the combat. It was said by a great gambler that the next pleasure in life to that of winning was that of losing; and to the real lover of whist, the next pleasure to that of playing a good game is that of looking on at one.

Whist has been extolled, and justly, upon many accounts; but the peculiar advantage of the game is, perhaps, that it utilises socially many persons who would not otherwise be attractive. Unless a player is positively disagreeable, he is as good to play whist with as a conversational Crichton. Moreover, though the poet has hinted of the evanescent character of 'friendships made in wine,' such is not the case with those made at whist. The phrase, 'my friend and partner,' used by a well-known lady in fiction, in speaking of another lady, is one that is particularly applicable to this social science, and holds good, as it does, alas, in no other case, even when the partner becomes an adversary.

RELATIONS.

It is a favourite utterance of a much 'put-upon' Paterfamilias of my acquaintance, when he finds his family more than usually too much for him, and cynically confesses his own shortcomings, that 'children cannot be too particular in their choice of their parents, or begin their education too early.'

But not only are children a necessity—that is, if the world of men and women is to be kept going, concerning the advantage of which there seems, however, just now, to be some doubt,—but when they have arrived, they cannot, except in very early life, be easily got rid of. In this respect they differ from the relations whose case I am about to consider, and also possess a certain claim upon us over and above the mere tie of blood, since we are responsible for their existence. The obligation on the other side is, I venture to think, a little exaggerated. If there is such a thing as natural piety, which, even in these days, few are found to deny, it is the reverence, it is true, with which children regard their parents; but their moral indebtedness to them as the authors of their being is open to doubt. That theory, indeed, appears to be founded upon false premises; for, unless in the case of an ancestral estate, I am not aware that the existence of children is much premeditated. On the contrary, their arrival is often looked upon, from pecuniary reasons, with much apprehension, or, at best, till they do arrive, they may be described, in common phrase, as 'neither born nor thought of.' I am a father myself, but I wish to be fair and to take a just view of matters. If a mother leaves her child on a doorstep, for example, the filial bond can hardly be expected to be very strong. In such a case, indeed, the infant seems to me to have a very distinct grievance against its female parent, and to be under no very overwhelming obligation to its father. 'Handsome is as handsome does' is a principle that applies to all relations of life, including the nearest; and if duty never absolutely ceases to exist, it is, at all events, greatly moulded by circumstances.

Patriotism, for instance, is very commendable, but your country must be worth something to make you love it. It is next to impossible that an inhabitant of Monaco, for example, should be patriotic. He can at most be only parochial. The love of one's mother is probably the purest and noblest of all human affections; but some people's mothers are habitual drunkards, and others professional thieves. Even filial reverence, it is plain, must stop somewhere. That is one of the objections which, with all humility, I feel to the religion of M. Comte. The worship of my grandmother would be impossible to me, unless I had reason to believe her to have been a respectable person. Her relationship, unless I had had the advantage of her personal acquaintance, would weigh I fear, but little with me, and that of my great-grandmother nothing at all. The whole notion of ancestry—unless one's ancestors have been distinguished people—seems to me ridiculous. If they have *not* been distinguished people—folks, that is, of whom some record has been preserved—how is one to know that they have been worthy persons, whose mission has been to increase the sum of human happiness? If, on the other hand, they have been only notorious, and done their best to decrease it, I should be most heartily ashamed of them. The pride of birth from this point of view—which seems to me a very reasonable one—is not only absurd, but often very reprehensible. We may be exulting, by proxy, in successful immorality, or even crime. Our boastfulness of our progenitors is necessarily in most cases very vague, because we know so little about them. When we come to the particular, the record stops very short indeed—generally at one's grandmother, who, by the way, plays a part in the dream-drama of ancestry little superior to that of that 'rank outsider,' a mother-in-law. 'Tell that to your grandmother' is a phrase that certainly did not originate in reverence; and even when that lady is proverbially alluded to in a complimentary sense, her intelligence is only eulogised in connection with the 'sucking of eggs.'

It so happens that I have quite a considerable line of ancestors myself, but only one of them ever distinguished himself, and that (he was an Attorney-General) in a doubtful way; and I confess I don't take the slightest interest in them. I prefer the pleasant companion with whom I came up in the train yesterday, and whose name I forgot to ask, to the whole lot of them.

And if I don't care about ancestors on canvas (for their pictures, of course, are all we have seen of them), I have good cause to be offended with them on paper. My favourite biographies—such as that of Walter Scott, for example—are disfigured by them. When men sit down to write a great man's life, why should they weary us with an epitome of that of his grandfather and grandmother? Of course, the book has to be a certain length. No one is more sensible than myself of the difficulty of providing 'copy' sufficient for two octavo volumes; but I do think biographers should confine themselves to two generations. For my part, I could do with one, but there is the favourite theory of a great man's inheriting his greatness from the maternal parent, which I am well aware cannot be dispensed with. It is like the white horse, or rather the grey mare, in Wouvermanns's pictures; you can't get rid of it any more than Mr. Dick could get Charles I. out of his memorial. For my part, I always begin biographies at the fourteenth chapter (or thereabouts)—'The subject of this memoir was born,' etc.; and even so I find I get quite enough of them. In novels the introduction of ancestry is absolutely intolerable. When I see that hateful chapter headed 'Retrospective,' I pass over to the other side, like the Levite, only quicker. What do I care whether our hero's grandfather was Archbishop of Canterbury or a professional body-snatcher? I don't even care which of the two was my own personal friend's grandfather, and how much less can I take an interest in this imaginary progenitor of the creation of an author's brain? The introduction of such a colourless shadow is, to my mind, the height of impertinence. If I were Mr. Mudie, I would put my foot down resolutely and stamp out this literary plague. As George III., who had an objection to commerce, is said to have observed, when asked to confer a baronetcy on one of the Broadwood family, 'Are you sure there is not a piano in it?' so should Mr. M. inquire of the publisher before taking copies of any novel, 'Are you sure there is not a grandfather in it?'

Again, what a nuisance is ancestry in our social life! It cannot, unhappily, be done away with as a fact, but surely it need not be a topic. How often have I been asked by some fair neighbour at a dinner-table, 'Is that Mr. Jones opposite one of the Joneses of Bedfordshire?' One's first impulse is naturally to ask, 'What on earth is that to you or me?' But experience teaches prudence, and I reply with reverence, 'Yes, of Bedfordshire,' which, at all events, puts a stop to argument upon the matter. Moreover, she seems to derive some sort of mysterious satisfaction from the information, and it is always well to give pleasure.

A well-known wit was once in company with one of the Cavendishes, who had lately been to America, and was recounting his experiences. 'These Republican people have such funny names,' he said. 'I met there a man of the name of Birdseye.' 'Well, and is not that just as good as Cavendish?' replied the wit, who was also a smoker. But the remark was not appreciated.

Ancestral people do not, as a rule, appreciate wit; but, on the other hand, it must be admitted that this is not a defect peculiar to them alone. I once knew a man of letters who, though he had risen to wealth and eminence, was of humble descent, and had a weakness for avoiding allusion to it. His daughter married a man of good birth, but whose literary talents were not of a high order. This gentleman wrote a letter applying for a certain Government appointment, and expressed a wish for his father-in-law's opinion upon the composition. 'It's a very bad letter,' was the frank criticism the other made upon it. 'The writing is bad, the spelling is indifferent, the style is abominable. Good heavens! where are your relatives and antecedents?' 'If it comes to that,' was the reply, 'where are yours? For I never hear you speak about them.' Nor did he ever hear him, for his father-in-law never spoke another word to him.

Nothing, of course, can be more contemptible than to neglect one's poor relations on account of their poverty; but it is very doubtful whether the sum of human happiness is increased by our having so much respect for the mere tie of kindred, unaccompanied by merit. Other things being equal, it is obviously natural that one's near relatives should be the best of friends. But other things are not always equal. Indeed, a certain high authority (which looks on both sides of most questions) admits as much. 'There is a friend,' it says, 'that sticketh closer than a brother. The connection, with its consequences, is somewhat similar to a partnership in commercial life. If partners pull together, and are sympathetic, nothing can be more delightful than such an arrangement. The tie of business clenches the tie of social attraction. For myself, I am not commercial; but I envy the old firm of Beaumont and Fletcher, and the modern one of Erckmann and Chatrian. But if the members of the firm do *not* pull together? Then, surely the bond between them is most deplorable, and a divorce *a vinculo* should be obtained as soon as possible.

One of the greatest mistakes—and there are many—that we fall into from a too ready acknowledgment of the tie of kindred is the obligation we feel under to consort with relations with whom we have nothing in common. You may take such persons to the waters of affection, but you cannot make them drink; and the more you see of them the less they are likely to agree with you. Not once, nor twice, but fifty times, in a life experience that is becoming protracted, I have seen this forcible bringing together of incongruous elements, and the result has been always unfortunate. I say 'forcible,' because it has been rarely voluntary; now and then a strong, though, I venture to think, a mistaken sense of duty may lead a man to seek the society of one with whom he has nothing in common save the bond of race; but for the most part they are obeying the wishes of another —the sacred injunction, perhaps, of a parent on his death-bed. 'Be good friends,' he murmurs, 'my children,' not reflecting, in that supreme and farewell hour, how little things, such as prejudice, difference of political or religious opinions, conflicting interests, and the like, affect us while we are in this world, and how perilous it is to attempt to link like with unlike. I am quite certain that when relations do not, in common phrase, 'get on well with one another,' the best chance of their remaining friends is for them to keep apart. This is gradually becoming recognised by 'the common sense of most,' as we see by the falling-off in those family gatherings at Christmas, which only too often partook of the character of that assembly which met under the roof of Mr, Pecksniff, with the disastrous result with which we are all acquainted.

The more distant the tie of blood, the less reason, of course, there is to consider it; yet it is strange to see how even sensible men will welcome the

Good-for-nothing, who chance to be 'of kin' to them, to the exclusion of the Worthy, who lack that adventitious claim. The effect of this is an absolute immorality, since it offers a premium to unpleasant people, while it heavily handicaps those who desire to make themselves agreeable. To give a particular example of this, though upon a large scale, I might cite Scotland, where, making allowance for the absence of that University system, which in England is so strong a social tie, there are undoubtedly fewer friendships, in comparison, than there are with us; this I have no hesitation in attributing to clanship—the exaggeration of the family tie—which substitutes nearness for dearness, and places a tenth cousin above the most charming of companions, who labours under the disadvantage of being 'nae kin.'

Again, what is more common than to hear it said, in apology for some manifestly ill-conditioned and offensive person, that he is 'good to his family'? The praise is probably only so far deserved that he does not beat his wife nor starve his children; but, supposing even he treated them as he should do, and, moreover, entertained his ten-times removed cousins to dinner every Sunday, what is that to *me* who do not enjoy his unenviable hospitality? Let his cousins speak well of him by all means; but let the rest of the world speak as they find. I protest against the theory that the social virtues should limit themselves to the home circle, and still more, that they should extend to the distant branches of it to the exclusion of the world at large.

Of Howard, the philanthropist, it is said—and, I notice, said with a certain cynical pleasure—that, notwithstanding his universal benevolence, he behaved with severity ta his own son. I have not that intimate acquaintance with the circumstances which, to judge by the confidence of their assertions, his traducers possess, but I should be slow to believe, in the case of such a father, that the son did not deserve all he got, or was not forgiven even to the seventy times seventh offence. There is, however, no little want of reason in the ordinary acceptation of the term, 'loving forgiveness.' He must be a very morose man who does not forgive a personal injury, especially when there has been an expression of repentance for it; but there are offences which, quite independently of their personal sting, manifest in the offender a cruel or bad heart, and 'loving forgiveness' is in that case no more to be expected than that we should take a serpent who has already stung us to our bosom. 'It is his nature to,' as the poet expresses it, and if that serpent is my relative it is my misfortune, and by no means impresses me with a sense of obligation. Indeed, in the case of an offensive relation, so far from his having any claim to my consideration, it seems to me I have a very substantial grievance in the fact of his existence, and that he owes me reparation for it.

It is perhaps from a natural reaction, and is a sort of unconscious protest against the preposterous claims of kinship, that our connections by marriage are so freely criticised, and, to say truth, held in contempt. No one enjoins us to love our wife's relations, indeed, our own kindred are generally dead against them, and especially against her mother, to whom the poor woman very naturally clings. This is as unreasonable in the way of prejudice, as the other line of conduct is in the way of favouritism. It is, in short, my humble opinion that, if everyone stood upon his or her own merits, and was treated accordingly, this world of ours would be the better for it; and of this I am quite sure—it would have fewer disagreeable people in it. I am neither so patriotic nor so thorough-going as the American citizen, who, during the late Civil War, came to President Lincoln, and nobly offered to sacrifice on the altar of freedom 'all his able-bodied relations;' but I think that most of us would be benefited if they were weeded out a bit.

INVALID LITERATURE.

It has always struck me as a breach of faith in Charles Lamb to have published the fact that dear, 'rigorous' Mrs. Battle's favourite suit was Hearts: and is in my eyes, notwithstanding Mr. Carlyle's posthumous outburst, the only blot on his character. His own confession, though tendered with a blush, that there is such a thing as sick whist stands on totally different grounds; it is not a relaxation of principle, but an acknowledgment of a weakness common to human nature. One of the most advanced thinkers and men of science of our time has frankly admitted that his theological views are considerably modified by the state of his health; and if one's ideas on futurity are thus affected, it is no wonder that things of this world wear a different appearance when viewed from a sick bed. It is not difficult to imagine that whist, for example, played on the counterpane by three good Samaritans, to while away the hours for an afflicted friend, differs from the game when played on a club card-table. Common humanity prevents our saying what we think of the play of an invalid who may be enjoying his last rubber; and if the ace of trumps *is* found under his pillow, we only smile and hope it will not occur again.

On the other hand, literary taste would, one would think, be the last thing to vary with our physical condition; yet those who have had long illnesses know better, and will, I am sure, bear me out in the assertion that there are such things as sick books. I do not, of course, speak of devotional works. I am picturing the poor man when he is getting well after a long bout of illness; his mind clear, but inert; his limbs painless, but so languid that they hardly seem to belong to him; and when he regards their attenuated proportions with the same sort of feeble interest that is evoked by eggshell china—they are not useful, still it would be a pity if they broke.

Then it is that one feels a loathing of the strong meats of literature, and a liking for its milk diet. As to metaphysics, one has had enough and to spare of *them* when one was delirious; while the 'Fairy Tales of Science' do not strike one just then as being quite so fairylike as the poet represents them. As to science, indeed, there is but one thing clear to us, namely, that the theory of evolution is a mistake; for though one's getting better at all is undoubtedly a proof of the survival of the fittest, we are well convinced that we have retrograded from what we were. It would puzzle Darwin himself to fix our position exactly, but though we lack the tenacity, and especially the colour, of the sea-anemone, we seem to be there or thereabouts in the scale of humanity. When last prostrated by rheumatic fever, or its remedies, I remember, indeed, to have been inclined to mathematics. When very ill I had suffered agonies in my dreams from the persecutions of an impossible quantity, and perhaps the association of ideas suggested, as I slowly gathered strength, a little problem in statics. It had been taught me by my dear tutor at Cambridge, whom undergraduates have long ceased to trouble, as a proof of the pathos that dwells in figures; and I kept repeating it to myself, with the letters all misplaced, till I became exhausted by tears and emotion.

As a general rule, however, even mathematics fail to interest the convalescent. 'Man delights not him; no, nor woman neither;' but Literature, if light in the hand, and always provided that he has his back to the window, is a pleasure to him only next to that of his new found appetite and his first chicken. His taste 'has suffered a sick change,' but that by no means implies it has deteriorated. On the contrary, his critical faculty has fled (which is surely an immense advantage), while he has recovered much of that power of appreciation which rarely abides with us to maturity. He is not on the outlook for mistakes, slips of style, anachronisms; he derives no pleasure from the discovery of spots in the sun, but is content to bask in the rays of it. He does not necessarily return to the favourites of his youth, though he has a tendency that way, but the shackles of convention have slipped away from him with his flesh, and he reads what he likes, and not what he has been told he ought to like. He has been so long removed from public opinion, that, like a shipwrecked crew in an open boat, it has ceased to affect him; only, instead of taking to cannibalism, he takes to what is nice. As his physical appetite is fastidious, so his mental palate has a relish only for titbits. If ever there was a time for a reasonable being to 'dip' into books, or to enjoy 'half-hours with the best authors,' this is it; but weak as the patient is, he commonly declines to have his tastes dictated to; perhaps there is an unpleasant association in his mind, arising from Brand and Liebig, with all 'extracts;' but, at all events, those literary compilations oppress and bewilder him; he objects to the extraordinary fertility of 'Ibid,' an author whose identity he cannot quite call to mind, and prefers to choose for himself.

Biography is out of the question. Long before he has got through that account of the hero's great grandmother, from whom he inherited his talents, which is, it seems, indispensable to such works, he yawns, and devoutly wishing, notwithstanding its fatal consequences to the fourth generation, that that old woman had never been born, falls into fitful slumber.

Travels are in the same condemnation; he has not the patience to watch the traveller taking leave of his family at Pimlico, or to follow his cab as he drives through the streets to the railway station, or to share the discomforts of his cabin—all necessary, no doubt, to his eventual arrival in Abyssinia, but hardly necessary to be described. Moreover, the convalescent has probably travelled a good deal on his own account during the last few weeks, for the bed of fever carries one hither and thither with the velocity, though not the ease, of the enchanted carpet in the 'Arabian Nights.' The desire of the sick man is to escape from himself and all recent experiences.

He thinks he will try a little History. Alison? No, certainly not Alison. 'They will be proposing Lingard next,' he murmurs, and the little irritation caused by the well-meant suggestion throws him back for the next six hours. Presently he tries Macaulay, whom some flatterer has fulsomely called 'as good as a novel,' but, though the trial of Warren Hastings gives him a fillip, the rout of Sedgemoor does away with the effect of it, and, happening upon the character of Halifax, he suffers a severe relapse. As a bedfellow, Macaulay is too declamatory, though, at the same time, strange to say, he does not always succeed in keeping one awake. To the sick man Carlyle is preferable; not his 'Frederick,' of course, and still less his 'Sartor Resartus,' which has become a nightmare, without head or tail, but his 'French Revolution.' One lies and watches the amazing spectacle without effort, as though it were represented on the stage. The sea of blood rolls before our eyes, the roar of the mob sounds in our ears; we are carried along with the unhappy Louis to the very frontier, and just on the verge of escape are seized and brought back—King Coach—with him to Paris, in a cold perspiration.

Some people, when in health and of a sane mind (Mr. Matthew Arnold one *knows* of, and there may be others), take great delight in 'Paradise Regained;' all we venture to say is that in sickness it does not suggest its title. It is said that barley-water goes well with everything; if so, the epic is the exception which proves the rule. Milton is tedious after rheumatic fever, Spencer is worse.

'"Not from the grand old masters,

Not from the bards sublime,

Whose distant footsteps echo

Through the corridors of Time,"'

murmurs the invalid, 'I can't stand them.' He does not mean anything depreciatory, but merely that—

'Like strains of martial music

Their mighty thoughts suggest

Life's endless toil and endeavour,'

which he is not fit even to think of. He cannot read Keats's 'Nightingale,' but for quite another reason. What arouses 'thoughts too deep for tears' in the hale and strong is to the sick as the sinking for an artesian well. 'The Chelsea Waterworks,' as Mr. Samuel Weller observed of Mr. Job Trotter (at a time when the metropolitan water supply would seem to have been more satisfactory than at present), 'are nothing to him.' On the other hand, Shelley's 'Skylark,' and the 'Dramatic Fragments' of Browning, are as cordials to the invalid, while the poems of Walter Scott are like breezes from the mountains and the sea. In that admirable essay, 'Life in the Sick-room,' the authoress justly remarks, speaking of the advantage of objectivity in sick books, 'Nothing can be better in this view than Macaulay's "Lays," which carry us at full speed out of ourselves.'

But it is not always that the invalid can read the poets at all; like Mrs. Wititterley, his nerves are too delicately strung for the touch of the muse. His chief enjoyment lies in fiction, to the producers of which he can never feel too grateful. I remember, on one occasion when I was very reduced indeed, taking up 'Northanger Abbey,' and reading, with almost the same gusto as though I had been a novelist myself, Miss Austen's defence of her profession. She says:

'I will not adopt that ungenerous and impolitic custom, so common with novel-writers, of degrading by their contemptuous censure the very performances to the number of which they are themselves adding, joining with their greatest enemies in bestowing the harshest epithets on such works, and scarcely even permitting them to be read by their own heroine, who, if she accidentally takes up a novel, is sure to turn from its insipid pages with disgust. Let us not desert one another; we are an injured body. Although our productions have afforded more extensive and unaffected pleasure than those of any other literary corporation in the world, no species of composition has been so much decried. From pride, ignorance, or fashion, our foes are almost as many as our readers; and while the abilities of the nine-hundred-and-ninety-ninth abridger of the history of England are eulogised by a thousand pens, there seems a general agreement to slight the performances which have only genius, wit, and taste to recommend them.'

I had quite forgotten till I came upon this passage that Miss Austen had such 'a kick in her,' and I remember how I honoured her for it and sympathised with her sentiments. 'When pain and anguish wring the brow,' we all know who is the comforter; but next to her, and when the brow is getting a little better, we welcome the novelist.

With our face aslant on the pillow, we once more make acquaintance with the characters that have been the delight of our youth, and find they delight us still, but with a difference. The animal spirits of Smollett and Fielding are a little too much for us; there is not sympathy enough in them for our own condition; they seem to have been fellows who were never ill. Perhaps 'Humphrey Clinker,' though it drags at the end, and the political disquisitions are intolerable, is the funniest book that ever was written; but the faculty of appreciation for it is not now in us. We turn with relief to Scott, though not to 'Scott's Works,' in the sense in which the phrase is generally used, as though they were a foundry from which everything is issued of the same workmanship and excellence; whereas there is as much difference between them as there was in her Majesty's ships of old between the gallant seventy-four and the crazy troopship. The invalid, however, as I have said, is far from critical; he only knows what he likes. Judged by this fastidious standard, he finds 'Waverley' somewhat wearisome, and, as to the first part of it in particular, wonders, not that the Great Unknown should have kept it in his desk for years as a comparative failure, but that he should have ever taken it from that repository. 'The Antiquary,' which in health he used to admire, or think he did, exceedingly, has also a narcotic effect; but 'Rob Roy' revives him, and 'Ivanhoe' stirs him like a trumpet-call.

What is very curious, just as the favourite literature of a cripple is almost always that which treats of force and action, so upon our sick-bed we turn most gladly to scenes of heroism and adventure. The famous ride in 'Geoffrey Hamlyn,' where the fate of the heroine, threatened with worse than death from the bush-rangers, hangs upon the horse's speed, seems to us, as we lie abed, one of the finest episodes in fiction. 'Tom Cringle's Log,' too, becomes a great favourite, not more from its buoyancy and freshness than from the melodramatic scenes with which it is interspersed.

In some moods of the sick man's mind, his morbid appetite tends, strange to say, to horrors. He 'snatches a fearful joy' from the weird and supernatural. I have known those terrible tales of Le Fanu, entitled 'In a Glass Darkly,' which for dramatic power and eeriness no other novelist has ever approached, devoured greedily by those whose physical sustenance has been dry toast and arrowroot.

The works of Thackeray are too cynical for the convalescent; he is for the present in too good a humour with destiny and human nature to enjoy them. He prefers the more cheerful aspects of life, and resents the least failure of poetic justice.

Taking the tenants of the sick ward all round, indeed, I have little doubt that the large majority would give their vote for Dickens. His pathos, it is true, is too much for them. Their hearts are as waxen as though Mrs. Jarley herself had made them. They are just in the condition to be melted by 'Little Nell,' and overcome by the death of Paul Dombey. They read 'David Copperfield' with avidity, but are careful to avoid the catastrophe of Dora and even the demise of her four-footed favourite. The book that suits them best is 'Martin Chuzzlewit.' Its genial comedy, quite different from the violent delights of 'Pickwick,' is well adapted to their grasp; while its tragedy, the murder of Montague Tigg—the finest description of the breaking of the sixth commandment in the language—leaves nothing to be desired in the way of excitement. But here we stray beyond our bounds, for 'Martin Chuzzlewit' is not a 'sick book;' or rather, it is one of the very few productions of human genius on the merits of which the opinions of both Sick and Sound are at one.

WET HOLIDAYS.

Even poets when they are on their travels feel the depressing influence of bad weather. Those lines of the Laureate—

'But when we crossed the Lombard plain,

Remember what a plague of rain—

Of rain at Reggio, at Parma,

At Lodi rain, Piacenza rain,'

are not among his best, but they evidently come from his very heart. When he used prose upon that journey his language was probably stronger. It is no wonder, then, that ordinary folks who have only a limited time in which to enjoy themselves, free from the fetters of toil, resent wet days. They are worst of all when we are touring on the Continent, where it is a popular fallacy to suppose the skies are always smiling, but at home they are bad enough. In Scotland, nobody but a Scotchman believes in fine weather, and consequently there is no disappointment; in England the Lake District is, perhaps, the most unfortunate spot for folks to be caught in by rain, because if there is no landscape there is nothing. *Spectare veniunt*, and when there are only the ribs and lining of their umbrellas to look at, their lot is hard indeed.

Wastwater is a charming place in sunshine—almost the only locality in England where things are still primitive and pastoral; but in rain! I hate exhibitions, but rather than Wastdale in wet weather, give me a panorama. Serious people may talk of 'the Devil's books,' but even a pack of cards, with somebody to play with you, is better under such circumstances than no book.

There is no limit to what human beings may be driven to by stress of weather, and especially by that 'clearing shower,' by which the dwellers in Lakeland are wont euphemistically to describe its continuous downpours. The Persians have another name for it—'the grandmother of all buckets.' I was once in Wastdale with a dean of the Church of England, respectable, sedate, and a D.D. It had poured for days without ceasing; the roads were under water, the passes were impassable, the mountains invisible; there was nothing to be seen but waterfalls, and those in the wrong place; there was no literature; the dean's guide-books were exhausted, and his Bible, it is but charitable and reasonable to suppose, he knew by heart. As for me, I had found three tourists who could play at whist, and was comparatively independent of the elements; but that poor ecclesiastic! For the first few days he occupied himself in remonstrating against our playing cards by daylight; but on the fourth morning, when we sat down to them immediately after breakfast, he began to take an enforced interest in our proceedings. Like a dove above the dovecot, he circled for an hour or two about the table—a deal one, such as thimble-riggers use, borrowed, under protest, from his own humble bedroom—and then, with a murmurous coo about the weather showing no signs of clearing up, he took a hand. Constant dropping—and it was much worse than dropping—will wear away a stone, and it is my belief if it had gone on much longer his reverence would have played on Sunday.

The spectacle that the roads of the district present at such a time is most melancholy. Everyone is in a closed car—a cross between a bathing machine and that convenient vehicle which carries both corpse and mourners; all the windows seem made of bottle glass, a phenomenon produced by the flattening of the noses of imprisoned tourists; and nothing shines except an occasional traveller in oilskin. In such seasons, indeed, oilskin (lined with patience) is your only wear. Ordinary waterproofs in such a climate become mere blotting paper, and with the best of them, without leggings and headgear to match, the poor Londoner might, I do not say just as well be in London (for that is his aspiration all day long), but just as well go to bed at once, and stop there. 'But why does he not go home?' it may be asked: a question to which there are several answers. In the first place (for one must take the average in such cases) because he is a fool. Secondly, like the rest of the well-to-do world, he has suffered the summer, wherein warmth and sunshine are really to be had, to slip by, and has only the fag end of it in which to take holiday. It is now or never—or at all events now or next year—with him. All his friends, too, are out of town, flattening *their* noses against window panes; his club is under repair, his house in brown holland, his servants on board wages. Like the young gentleman in Locksley Hall, he is so absolutely at the end of his resources, that an 'angry fancy' is all that is left to him. Of course, under its influence he sits down and writes to the *Times*; but, if the humblest of its correspondents may venture to say so without offence, even that does not help him much. That suicides increase in wet autumns is notorious; but that murders should in these sequestered vales maintain the even tenor of their way is a feather in the cap of human nature. In lodgings, where the pent-up tourist has no one but his wife and family to speak to, where Dick and Tom *will* romp in his only sitting-room, and Eliza Jane practises all day on the crazy piano, this forbearance is especially creditable.

Even in hotels, however, there is great temptation. On the north-eastern coast, in particular, when the weather has, as the phrase goes, 'broken up,' and the sky and sea have both become one durable drab, the best of women grow irritable, the men morose. At the *table d'hôte*, which even the most exclusive are driven to frequent for company, as sheep huddle together in storm, Dislike ripens to Hate with frightful rapidity. Our neighbour, who always—for it seems always—gets the last of the mushrooms at breakfast, or finishes the oyster sauce at dinner before our very eyes, we are very far, indeed, from loving as ourselves. Our *vis-à-vis*, the man on his honeymoon, is even still more offensive. We resent his happiness, which is apparently uninfluenced by the state of the weather, and our wife wonders what he could have seen in that chit of a girl to attract his attention. To ourselves she seems a great deal too good for him, and in our rare intervals of human feeling we regard her with the tenderest commiseration. The importance attached to meals, and the time we take over them, have no parallel save among the Esquimaux. The least incident that happens in the hotel is of more moment to us than the overthrow of Empires. The whispered news that a fellow guest has been taken seriously ill, and that a medical consultation has been held upon the case, is a matter to be deplored, of course, but one which is not without its consolations. 'Who is it? What is it? Nothing catching I do hope?' (this last uttered with genuine anxiety) are questions that are heard on every side. The general impression is that some lovely young lady of fashion on the drawing-room floor has been seized with pains in her limbs—and no wonder—from exposure to the elements. Her mother comes down every morning and selects dainties for the sick-room from the public breakfast table; those who are near enough to do so inquire in dulcet tones, 'How is your invalid this morning?' The reply is, 'Better, much better,' which somehow falls short of expectation. Even the most giddy and frivolous of girls has no excuse for frightening people for nothing.

At luncheon one day a very fat, strong boy makes his appearance, and is supplied with soup. All his neighbours who have no soup are wild with envy, though they are well acquainted with that soup at dinner, and know that it is bad. 'What is the meaning of it? Why this favouritism?' we inquire of the waiter furiously. 'Well, you see, sir, he is better now; but that is the invalid.' The delicate, attractive creature we have pictured to ourselves with pains in her limbs turns out, after all, to be a hulking schoolboy, probably bilious from over-eating. The public indignation is excessive, while the subject of it, quite unconscious of the fact, has another plate of soup.

The wild weather out of doors is not, of course, confined to the land, and the sea would be a fine sight if it was not invisible. The waves, indeed, are so high that the fishing-boats which have remained out all night are often warned off, or, as it is locally termed, 'burned off,' from the harbour bar. A tar barrel is lighted for this purpose on the headland, and it is the only thing which the eternal rain cannot utterly squelch and extinguish. Occasionally we venture down upon the pier to see the boats make the harbour, which, not a little to our disappointment, they never fail to do. There are huge buttresses of stone against the pier-head, behind which the new comer imagines he may crouch in perfect safety, till the third wave comes in and convinces him to the contrary. No one ever dreams of 'burning' *him* off—giving him one word of warning of that unpleasant contingency; for to behold a fellow creature more drenched and dripping than ourselves is very soothing. As to the dangers of maritime life, we are all agreed that they are greatly overrated; and some sceptics even go so far as to suggest that the skeleton ship, half embedded in the sands, which so impresses visitors in fine weather, is not a genuine wreck at all, but has been placed there by the Town Corporation to delude the public.

Now and then we splash down to the quay to see a few million of herrings sold at four shillings a hundred, which will presently induce philanthropic fishmongers in London to advertise 'a glut this morning,' and to retail them at threepence apiece. At rare intervals we explore the dripping town. It is amazing what a fascination the small picture-shops, to which at home we should never give a glance, afford us; even the frontispieces to popular music have unwonted attractions; while the pottery-shops, full of ware made from clay 'peculiar to the locality,' are only too seductive to our wives, who purchase largely what they believe to be great bargains, till they find on their return home the identical articles in Oxford Street, at half the price. In London we never visit the British Museum itself, unless to escort some country cousin, but at Barecliff-on-Sea, in wet weather, the miserable little local Institute, with its specimens of strata, its calf with two heads in spirits, and its petrified toad, is an irresistible temptation. The great event of the day, however, is the wading down to the railway-station (which is in a quagmire) to meet the express train which brings more victims, 'unconscious of their doom,' to Barecliff, and who evidently flatter themselves that the pouring rain is an exceptional phenomenon; it also brings the London newspapers, for which we fight and struggle (the demand being greatly in excess of the supply) and think ourselves fortunate if we secure a supplement. It is true there is a *Times* in the smoking-room of the hotel, but it is always engaged five deep, is the cause of terrible quarrels, and every afternoon we expect to see it imbrued in gore.

In the evening, when one does not mind the wet so much—'its tooth is not so keen because it is not seen'—there are dissipations at 'the Rooms by the Sea.' Amateur charitable concerts are given there, in which it is whispered that this and that lady at the *table d'hôte* will take part, who become public characters and objects of immense interest in consequence. Thither, too, come 'the inimitable Jones,' from the Edgware Road Music Hall, with his 'unrivalled *répertoire* of comic songs;' the Spring Board Family, who have been 'pronounced by the general consensus of the medical faculty in London to be unique,' as having neither joints nor backbone; and Herr von Deft, 'who will repeat the same astounding performances which have electrified the reigning families of Europe.' The serious people (for whom 'the glee-singers of Mesopotamia' are also suspected of dropping a line) are angled for by white-cravatted lecturers, who enhance their statistics of conversion by the exhibition of poisoned arrows, and of clubs, on which, with the microscope, may be detected the hairs of missionary martyrs. In fine weather, of course, these attractions would be advertised in vain; but the fact is, our whole community has been reduced by the cruelty of the elements to a sort of second childhood; the rain which permeates everything is softening our brain.

This is only too evident from the conversation in the hotel porch where the men meet every morning to discuss the topic of the day—the weather. A sullen gloom pervades them—the first symptom of mental aberration. Those, on the other hand, who express their opinion that it 'really seems to be clearing a little' are in more advanced stages. We who are less afflicted shake our heads, and murmur painfully, but also with a considerable touch of contempt, 'Poor fellows!'

The piano in the ladies' drawing-room is always going, but it excites no soothing influence; there is an impression in the hotel that the performers are foreigners, and should be discouraged. But there is one instrument hanging in the hall on which everyone plays, native or alien, and every note is discord. It is the barometer. People talk of the delicacy of scientific instruments; if they are right, the shocks which that barometer survives proves it to be an exception. Batter it as we may, and do, the faithful needle, with a determination worthy of a better cause, maintains its position at 'Much Rain.' The manager is appealed to vehemently, coarsely; he shrugs his shoulders, protests with humility that he cannot help the weather, or affirms it is unprecedented—which we do not believe. Other managers—in the Engadine, for example—the papers say, are providing excellent weather; what does he mean by it?

At last one morning, wetter than ever, some noble spirit, the Tell of our liberties, exclaims, 'Who would be free, himself must strike the blow.' His actual words (if one was not writing history) are, 'Hang me if I stand this any longer,' and they strike the keynote of everybody's thought. He goes away by the next train, and his departure is followed by the same effects as the tapping of a reservoir. The hotel company—I mean the inmates; the company goes into bankruptcy—stream off at once to their own homes.

That journey through the pouring rain is the happiest day of our wet holiday. How beautiful looms soaking, soppy, smoky London! In that excellent town who cares for rain?

'Blow, winds, and crack your cheeks! rage! blow!

You cataracts and hurricanoes spout.'

Pooh! pooh! Call a cab—call two!

TRAVELLING COMPANIONS.

It was held by wise men of old that adversity was the test of friendship, but as his Excellency the Minister of the United States has observed, *per* Mr. Biglow, 'They did not know everything down in Judee;' and among other subjects of which those ancient writers were necessarily ignorant was that of Continental travel. The coming to grief of a friend is unquestionably very inconvenient; as a millionaire of my acquaintance observes (under the influence, as he confidently believes, of benevolent emotion), 'One likes to see one's friends prosperous;' but even when they are not so, it requires some effort to follow the dictates of prudence and cast them off. And, after all, the man, even though you may cut him, remains the same; as fit for the purposes of friendship as ever, except for his pecuniary condition. There is no such change in his relation to oneself as Emerson describes in one of his essays; his words I forget, and his works are miles away, but the man he has in his mind has in some way fallen short of expectation—declined, perhaps, to lend the philosopher money. 'Yesterday,' he says, 'my friend was the illimitable ocean; to-day he is a pond.' He had come to the end of him. And some friends, as my little child complains as he strokes his black kitten, 'end so soon.'

There are no circumstances, however, under which friendship comes so often to a violent and sudden death as under the pressure of travel. It is like the fate which the Scientific ascribe to a box sunk in the sea; after a certain depth, which varies according to the strength of the box, the weight of the superincumbent water bursts it up. It is merely a question of how deep or how strong. Our travelling companion remains our friend for a day, for a week, for even a month; but at the month's end he is our friend no longer. Our relations have probably become what the diplomatists term 'strained' long before that date, but a day comes when the tension becomes intolerable; the cable parts and we lose him. Unfortunately, not always, however; there are circumstances—such as being on board ship, for example—when we thus part without parting company. A long voyage is the most terrible trial to which friendship can be subjected. It is like the old sentence of pressing to death, 'as much as he can bear, and more.' It is doubtful, for example, whether friendship has ever survived a voyage to Australia. I have sometimes asked a man whether he knew So-and-So, who hails, like himself, from Melbourne, and he has replied, 'We came over in the same ship'—'Only that, and nothing more,' as the poet puts it; but his tone has an unmistakable significance, and one perceives at once that the topic had better not be pursued.

A very dear friend of mine once proposed that we should go round the world together; he offered to pay all my expenses, and painted the expedition in rose-colour. But I had the good sense to decline the proposal. I felt I should lose my friend. Even yachting is a very dangerous pastime in this respect, especially when the vessel is becalmed. In that case, like the sea itself, one's friend soon becomes a pond. Conceive, then, what it must be to go round the world with him! Is it possible, both being human, that we can still love one another when we have got to Japan, for instance? And then we have to come back together! How frightful must be that moment when he tells us the same story he told at starting, and we feel that he has come to the end of his tether, and is going to tell *all* his stories over again! This is why it so often happens that only one of two friends returns from any long voyage they have undertaken together. What has become of the other? A question that one should never put to the survivor. It is certain that great travellers, and especially those who travel by sea, have a very different code of morals from that which they conform to at home. Human life is not so sacred to them. Perhaps it is in this respect that travel is said to enlarge the mind. That it does not sharpen it, however, whatever it may do for the temper, is tolerably certain. In their habits travellers are singularly conventional. They are compelled, of course, to suffer certain inconveniences, but they endure others, and most serious ones, quite unnecessarily, merely because it is the custom so to do. In crossing the Atlantic, for example, a man of means will submit to be shut up in a close cupboard for ten days with an utter stranger, though by paying double fare he can get a cabin to himself. This arises from no desire for economy, but simply because he does not think for himself; other travellers do the like, and he follows their example. Yet what money could recompense him for occupying for the same time *on land* a double-bedded room—not to say a mere china closet—with a man of whom he knows nothing except that he is subject to chronic sickness? A pleasant sort of travelling companion indeed, yet, strange to say, the commonest of all. Where there is a slender purse this terrible state of things (supposing travel under such circumstances to be compatible with pleasure at all, which, for my part, I cannot imagine) is not a matter of choice; but where it can be avoided why is it undergone?

There is nothing that convinces me of the folly of mankind so much as those advertisements we see in the summer months with respect to travelling companions, from volunteers of both sexes: 'Wanted, a travelling companion for a few months on the Continent, etc. The highest references will be required.' The idea of going with a stranger upon a tour of pleasure must surely originate in Hanwell, and the adventurer may think himself fortunate if it does not end in Broadmoor. References, indeed! Who can answer for a fellow-creature's temper, patience, unselfishness, during such an ordeal as a protracted tour? No one who has not travelled with him already; and one may be tolerably certain his certificate does not come from *that* quarter. It is true some people are married to strangers by advertisement; but their companionship, as I am given to understand, does not generally last for months, or anything like it.

Imagine two people, as utterly unknown to one another, except by letter (and 'references'), as the *x* and *y* of an equation, meeting for the first time at the railway-station! With what tremors must each regard the other! What a relief it must be to X. to find that Y. is at least a white man; on the other hand, it must rather dash his hopes, if they are set on pedestrianism, to find that his *compagnon de voyage* has a wooden leg. Yet what are his mere colour and limbs compared with his temperament and disposition? If one did not know the frightful risks one's fellow-creatures incur every day for little pleasure and less profit, one would certainly say these people must be mad.

But if instead of X. and Y., it is even A. and B., men who have known one another for years, and in every relation but as fellow-travellers, there is risk enough in such a venture. One night, after dinner at the club, they agree with effusion to take their autumn trip together; they are warm with wine and with the remembrance of their college friendship—which extended perhaps, when they afterwards come to think about it, a very little way. What days they will have in Switzerland together! What mornings (to see the sunrise) upon mountain-tops! What evenings on Lucerne! What nights in Paris! A. thinks himself fortunate indeed in having secured B.'s society for the next three months—a man with such a reputation for conversation; even T., the cynic of the club, has testified to his charm of manner. By-the-bye, what was it—exactly—T. had said of B.? A. cannot remember it at the moment, but recalls it on the night before they start together. 'B. is a charming fellow, only he has this peculiarity—that if there is only one armchair in a room, B. is sure to get it.'

B., on the other hand, congratulates himself on A.'s excessive good sense, which even T. had knowledged. What was it—exactly—T. had said of A.? He cannot remember it at the moment, but recalls it on the night before they start together. 'A. is such a thoroughly practical fellow; he has committed many follies, and not a few crimes, but he can lay his hand on the place where his heart should be, and honestly aver that he has never given sixpence to anybody.' Full of misgivings, and with demonstrations of satisfaction that are in themselves suspicious, they meet at the terminus. A. has a little black bag, which contains his all; it frees him from all trouble about luggage, and (especially) from the necessity of paying a porter. He is resolved not to lose a moment, nor spend a sixpence, in a Custom-house. To his horror, he perceives that B., whose one idea is comfort, has a portmanteau specially designed for him (apparently upon the model of Noah's Ark), and which can scarcely be got into the luggage-van. This article delays them twenty-four hours at every frontier, because the ordinary authorities decline to open it upon the ground that it contains an infernal machine, and have to telegraph to their Government for instructions.

Again, B. is no doubt a charming conversationalist—in English; but he does not know one single word of any other language. He requires every observation of their alien fellow-travellers to be translated, and then says 'Oh!' discontentedly, or 'It seems to me that foreigners have no ideas.' And not for one moment can A. get rid of him. If there *is* a friend that sticketh closer than a brother, it is the Travelling Companion who is dependent upon you for interpretation. It is needless to say that under these circumstances the glass of Friendship falls from 'Set Fair' to 'Stormy' with much rapidity. After A's fourth quarrel with a waiter about half a franc, B. calls him a 'mean hound,' and takes the opportunity of returning to his native land with a French count, who speaks perfect English, and robs him of his watch and chain and the contents of his pocket-book on board the steamer. A. and B. meet one another daily at the club for years afterwards, but without recognition.

Their case, of course, is an extreme one; but that of C. and D. is almost as bad. They are men of prudence, and persuade E. to go with them, as a makeweight. 'If we should ever disagree,' they say, 'as to what is to be done—which, however, is to the last degree improbable—the majority of votes shall carry it'—an arrangement which only delays the inevitable event—

'Three little nigger boys went the world to view,

The third was left in Calais, and then there were two.'

They find the makeweight intolerable before they have crossed the Channel, and, having agreed to cut their cable from him, are from that moment never in the same mind about anything else. It is a modern version of the three brigands who stole the Communion plate. C. and D. push E. over the precipice, and C. stabs D. at a supper for which D. has purveyed poisoned wine.

The only way to secure a really eligible travelling companion is to try him first in short swallow-flights, or rather pigeon-flights, from home. Take your bird with you for a few days' outing near home; then, if he proves pleasant, for a week's tour in Cornwall; then for ten days in Scotland, where, if you meet with the usual weather, and he still keeps his temper and politeness, you may trust yourself to him anywhere. Out of twenty failures there will, perhaps, be one success. In this manner I have discovered in time, in my dearest and nearest friends, the most undreamt of vices. One man, F., hitherto much respected as a Chancery barrister, has, as it has turned out, been intended by nature for a professional pedestrian. His true calling is to walk 'laps' round the Agricultural Hall or at Lillie Bridge, with nothing on to speak of save a handkerchief round his forehead. 'Let us walk' is his one cry as soon as he becomes a travelling companion. And he is not content to do this when he arrives at any place of interest, but insists upon walking *there*—perhaps along a dusty road, or over turnip-fields. I like walking myself in moderation—say a mile out and a mile in; but not, certainly not, twenty miles at a stretch, and at a speed which precludes conversation. This class of travelling companion is very dangerous. If he does not get his walking he becomes malignant. My barrister, at least, being denied the opportunity of drawing out marriage-settlements, conveying land, or otherwise plundering the community, took to practical jokes. Having a suspicion of his pedestrian powers, from the extreme length of his legs, I took G. with us, a man whom I could trust in that respect, and who fancied he had heart complaint. G. and I took our exercise alone together in a fly. One day we took a long drive—four miles or more—to a well-known bay. The vehicle could not get down to the sea, so we descended on foot, leaving it at the top of the cliff, with the strictest orders to the man not to stir till we came back. When we returned the fly was gone. How we reached our hotel, Heaven knows! but we did arrive there, in the last stage of exhaustion. The driver of the carriage, whom we met next day, informed us that a gentleman had been thrown from his horse on the cliff-top and had broken his leg, and that, under the circumstances, he had ventured to disobey our instructions and take the poor fellow home. Years afterwards I discovered that nothing of the kind had happened, but that the fiendish F. had given the driver a sovereign to play that trick upon us. F. is a judge now, and has been lately trying election cases. I wonder what he thinks of himself when he rebukes offenders for the heinous crime of bribery!

Again, I always thought H. a pleasant fellow till we went together to Cornwall. He had gone through the first ordeal of a few days nearer home to my satisfaction, but at Penzance he broke out. He was so dreadfully particular about his food that nothing satisfied him—not even pilchards three times a day; and the way he went on at the waiters is not to be described by a decent pen. The attendant at Penzance was not, I am bound to say, a good waiter. He said, though he habitually put his thumb in every dish, he 'hadn't quite got his hand in,' and was not used to the business.'

'Used! you know nothing about it!' exclaimed H., viciously. Then the poor fellow burst into tears. 'Pray be patient with me, good gentlemen,' he murmured. 'I do my best; but until last Wednesday as ever was I was a pork-butcher.' One cannot stand a travelling companion who makes the waiters cry.

The worst kind of fellow-traveller is one who, to use his own scientific phrase for his complaint, suffers from 'disorganisation of the nervous centres.' At home his little weaknesses do not strike you. You may not be on the spot when he flies across Piccadilly Circus, pursued, as he fancies, by a Brompton omnibus which has not yet reached St. James's Church, and is moving at a snail's pace; you may not have been with him on that occasion when, in his eagerness to be in time for the 'Flying Dutchman,' he arrives at Paddington an hour before it starts, and is put into the parliamentary train which is shunted at Slough to let the 'Dutchman' pass; but when you come to travel with him you know what 'nerves' are to your cost. On the other hand, this is the easiest kind of travelling companion to get rid of; for you have only to feign a sore throat, with feverish symptoms, and off he flies on the wings of terror, leaving you, as he thinks—if he *has* a thought except for his nervous centres—to the tender mercies of a foreign doctor, to hireling nurses, and to a grave in the strangers' cemetery.

THE END.

Milton Keynes UK
Ingram Content Group UK Ltd.
UKHW010758260424
441811UK00004B/368

9 789357 968812